BEN AND BERTHA BENJAMIN'S
Institute of *West African Spirituality*
Mission Statement
"Fighting for the definition of Black History"
Presents

QUESTIONS OF BLACK SALVATION/
BLACK HISTORY AND AFRICAN SOUL

Grass root Historians
Orchester Benjamin Sr. (Voice)
Linda Benjamin (Heart)
Clovis Benjamin-Dinwiddie (Soul)
Orchester Benjamin Jr. (Mind)

SoulViewWorld LLC/ Publishing
www.SoulViewWorld.com

Grandpa! Tell us a Story: Drinking from Ancient Wells:
Ancient West African Spirituality Series.
Questions of Black Salvation/Black History and African Soul

ISBN 978-0-9773421-3-6

SAN: 257-3326

Back Cover Photo taken by Marcus Benjamin

Book Cover Artwork © Orchester Benjamin

DEDICATION
To the memory my grandson
Orchester (Rory) Benjamin III,
Who gave me the name Hip-hop Grandpa.
Born February 14, 1986
Died of cancer April 21, 2007
To the memory of my Parents
Ben Jr. and Bertha Benjamin
To the memory of my Grandparents
Thomas, Georgia, and Arnolia Talton
Ben, Julie, and Judy Benjamin
To my sister, brothers, and their families
Clovis R. Brown
Ben Benjamin III
Walter M. Benjamin
And all members of my extended Family, living and dead
And to all of my grandchildren
And
Great Grandchildren

ACKNOWLEDGMENTS.

Family

I am deeply indebted to my daughter, Clovis Benjamin-Dinwiddie, for inspiring me to publish my story in the first place. My son, Orchester Benjamin Jr. who brought me back home, understands what I am doing, why, and helps me keep my head on straight on all levels; and my daughter-in-law, Norma Gooley-Benjamin, who gave me invaluable help, especially with the first draft of the manuscript. And my daughter, Linda Benjamin, whose assistance with my many rewrites and additions cannot be measured.

However, their help was limited grammar-wise, because of my belief that in order to be a "honest historian writer," I insisted on most grammar to remain exactly as I use words in my thinking-understanding process—somewhat Ebonic.

....

CONTENTS
Questions and Aspects of slavery

PROLOGUE
Kicking the Game around with my Grandsons
About Questions of Black Salvation

DionDi: "Grandpa, didn't you say that puberty is the time that a boy learns the things he needs to be a man. And when he reaches manhood, he will *create himself* into what he wants to be, and do in life?"

Marcus: "But wait a minute Grandpa, doesn't a man have to first *pull his mind together*, and then when he reaches manhood he can create himself into whatever he wants to be, and do in life?"

Michael: "Does that mean that before any of that can happen, doesn't he have to *choose what he wants* to be, and do in life?"

Tyree: "Then that leaves the question, how does a child know how to choose what he wants when he becomes a man, *if he doesn't already have his mind together?*"

Orchester Benjamin III: "That is right, when a child reaches *five or six years old, people begin to ask him what he wants to be when he grows up.* Grandpa can you tell us a **story about thinking for ourselves?**"

Grandpa: "The mind is *a question of survival answering machines*, and if you ask the right question, at the right time, your mind will automatically either think of the answer, or be able to recognize the answer when looking for it in the world. For example, when you say, "you know, there is some truth to what that person said."

The two and most important right questions a young man must ask himself is, what do I want, and how much am I going to pay for it? For example, each one of you *ask the right questions* for the problems you see facing you as a young man; *is my mind together enough to survive, and do what I want to do* in life? "*I want,*" are the key words.

The *right questions lead to the right answers.* The *problems arise in finding the right questions to ask yourself. The right questions are always related to what you want.* If you don't know what you want, *you will not find the right questions.* You have to keep in mind that, what you *want becomes your mission (chosen destiny) in life.* So the answer to your questions, is to *know what you want, and your mind will lead you to it.* The question become's, how to pay for it? **Bottom line; *successful thinking depends on how serious you are about what you want.***

For example, *I wanted* to teach my family Black history because it was not being taught in schools. At that moment, *my mission* in life was revealed to me, and I made a vow then and there, (*how I am going to pay for it?*) to become an **arm-chair Grass Roots Historian to teach my family the history of the Game, and an autobiographer to teach them the lessons I learned about living Life.** With that vow, I had chosen what I wanted, and knew how to (*pay for it*) achieve it.

From that point of view, I am going to tell you a little story about a speech I made to the Black Community, seeking the right questions about the *Salvation of Black people* in the twenty-first century. And the *problems* in the Black community, caused by *asking the wrong questions* about Black life, and history. And you will see how those questions became the point of departure of me becoming a Historian writing books; *paying the cost, there is no free ride.*

And when I finish, I want all of you to tell me if you see that asking the right questions is the pathway for your mind to follow in leading you to what you want. And also if it gave you any confidence that your mind will lead you to what you want.

Then check out what I have to say about the **Bibliography.**

QUESTIONS OF BLACK SALVATION/ BLACK HISTORY AND AFRICAN SOUL

(A)
Introduction and libation

Honored Brother and Sister Elders of the Black Community, my purpose for coming before you is two-fold. I want to present to you some of the major questions I found facing the Black community in the twenty first century.

In addition, at the end of my presentation, if you agree with me about the importance of the kind of questions mentioned, I am going to present the research method I used to seek answers to the Questions of Black Salvation, as well as a bibliography of my research sources. Including **a** list of all of the books I have written, or are in the pipe line. All of which are focused on answers to the Questions of Black Salvation; because, Sisters and Brothers, I am also a book/idea seller related to Black history.

Now with that said, in African Traditions, Women give birth, and nurture us as a people, and therefore, through childbirth, are the Owners of Black Society. As a salute to Black motherhood, I ask permission of our Sister Elders to pour libation for the Ancestors of their Society.

I pour this libation as a request for the presence of the Spirits of all of our Ancestors who were put on a slave ship in West and Western Central Africa, and ended up in what is called the United States of America; including all of their Descendants up to the present time.

The ones, whose blood, guts, bones, and strong desires for freedom are buried in American soil, and whose religious beliefs, hopes, dreams, joys, and sorrows, are buried in our Souls as part of our History. Especially, the spirits of the Tom Talton, and Ben Benjamin families, with a focus on Ben and Bertha Benjamin, my mother and father.

I seek permission to speak about you (our Ancestors) to your children, (Black Society) because our Elder Generation doesn't know, or have forgotten our inherited African Fortitude, Drive, and Determination. The way of thinking that you used to move mountains, cross rivers, and plant the Tree of Life by the poolside of Holy Water. This attitude is not being consciously taught to our younger generation for some reason or other. You, our beloved Ancestors, are being ignored at best, and hated at worst in their education, especially our most ancient Ancestors.

Ancestors come, eat, drink, and bear witness that the questions I bring forth to your people are *the right questions to turn the Black world right side up in our minds, because slavery has turned it upside down; which is Black people's Salvation*; Correct me if I half step!

(B)

Ancestor's worldview aspects

Now brothers and sisters, with our Ancestors sitting in the jury box, let's begin with the idea of Afro-Centralism; an idea that is having all kinds of ramifications on how some of us think about ourselves and our history.

For example: One of the things that emerged from Black's activities in the late 1950s, 60s, 70s, 80s, and into the 90s, was a much deeper awareness of the value of Black history.

This expanded awareness, accelerated by the book and T.V show Roots written by Alex Haley, which produced in Blacks a strong desire to know more about just what this history consisted of, and just as important, what purpose does an expanded awareness of history serve?

This led to lots of controversy and debates between, and within Black intellectual groups; especially Black historians and Preachers. Out of which came the idea that Black people are Afro-Centric in nature, and our soul has an African World View, and or, redefined Black Christianity to have an Afro-Centric Soul which began with Marcus Garvey in the 1920s. In this sense, I believe that all of our Brother and Sister Intellectuals, Historians, and Preachers are right, but shouldn't we take it further?

The words *Soul and Afro-Centric* are the terms that interest me most of all because, as a religious people, if clearly defined, aren't they the key to understanding the values of Black history? I will focus on questions about defining Afro-Centralism and see how it is related to Black history.

Shouldn't the definition of Afro-Centralism rest on the self-evident fact that every race of people in the world has their own way of thinking and doing things, called culture?

For example, isn't there a European way of thinking and doing things? Also, isn't there an Asian way of thinking and doing things; and a Hindu way of thinking and doing things? Isn't their way of thinking and doing things based on their worldview, called Euro-Centric, Hindu-Centric, and Asian-Centric World Views? Deep inside, no two people think and do things in the exact same way, or to say, have the same Worldview.

Especially in America; isn't this something we see every day around us, and is well known by the masses of Black people? Isn't it also a fact that Africans also have a unique way of thinking and doing things, and we can also see this around us, and is known by the masses of Black people? Therefore, can't we define an Afro-Centric World View to mean, an African way of thinking and doing things according to the way we see the world?

Following this definition, the question becomes, how is an African Tradition Intelligence way of thinking and doing things related to the values in Black history? Now isn't a World View important, because what you see, and how you see it, is the course you will pursue in life, i.e. how you live life? Isn't the way a people are living their lives over time the content of their history?

This means that I readily agree with Black historians and other Black intellectuals about the existence of an African World View as a way of seeing and understanding our history, and Black preachers defining our Soul that way. Yet I strongly disagree with them about their definition of what an African World View and Soul consists of, and how their definition relates to the Black experience of Black history.

The thing I think is missing from our way of thinking about history is what I call, a time line of human experiences. And this is because we don't ask ourselves the right questions.

The right question is, will understanding an African bush way of thinking and doing things lead to understanding Black America's spirituality? Is Black spirituality the key to understanding Black Soul? And is African Soul the key to understanding Black history? The foundation of our questions is our definition of an African World View, and the definitions involved, are the things I want to speak with you about.

Towards this end, my motivation for speaking to you is to provoke deep thinking along a series of questions concerning Black people's history and African Soul passed down to me from my mother and father and the Black community. Isn't the definition of an Afrocentric World View based on African traditional logic? Doesn't this lead to the question of how to use an African Bush way of thinking and doing things? Or, what I believe the even bigger question is, are Black people already using an African Bush way of thinking and doing things, and it is either unconscious or is being ignored?

We will call these, questions about an Afrocentric World View.

(C)

Right questions aspects

Now let's turn our attention to why I believe we are ignoring, or misusing what we already have i.e., logic of an African World View. It is a fact that we are Africans, and our Black minds are the most beautiful spiritually creative minds in the world. There is no question or problem we can't deal with. Doesn't our survival through slavery prove this beyond a doubt? Didn't we have to use our minds on its deepest level to survive Slavery?

However, we are allowing White people to define everything, and pose their questions to which we focus our minds, why? Now let's turn our attention to some examples of us allowing Whites to define questions for us to think about.

Do you doubt that we are in the position to have to prove to Whites that we are, in Jessie Jackson's words, "Somebody"? And at the same time, using White's way of thinking that defines us as "nobody;" the question becomes, are we somebody? If so, who are we? That is taking Brother Jessie out of context, but the point remains.

Our question should be, what qualifications do White people have that make us think that we can trust their judgment on defining how we should think about ourselves? Is it a case of being too lazy, or afraid to do our own thinking, and just allow Whites to do it for us?

The point being, isn't allowing White people, or anybody else to define what we think about empowers them to define the values leading to what is important in our life; who we are, the history of us as a people, and our traditional way of thinking about ourselves?

Can we really afford for this to happen when defining the African bush way of thinking and doing things, and still call it Afrocentric? What is wrong with letting the idea of Afrocentric define us? Their questions only lead us to following their European way of thinking that we are nobody.

For instance, is there any doubt that White people think Black people are inferior, and if Black people think like them, won't we think we are inferior? Whose fault is that? White people or us?

From an African Traditional point of view, is the question really about inferiority and superiority? Isn't this the chain that must be intellectually broken, if we are to be free to use an African Bush way of thinking, which some historians call Afro-centralism?

For still another example, aren't White's definitions of Blacks living south of the Sahara Desert (Tarzan movies), as well as our historical experience in America, viewed as not being one of history making, but only a state of Uncle Tom-ism, and African Traditional Religion as Pagan and not a religion at all?

Why should we allow those kinds of questions to capture our minds? Doesn't this allow White people to define the values contained in our African history as being of no value? And, are Black historians guided by their questions, reaching the same conclusions?

From this point of view, shouldn't we re-define history and religion? Aren't these the tools we need to define Black history from an African bush point of view? Are White people's questions the most important historical questions confronting Black people today?

I believe that using the intelligence in African bush thinking, and asking the right questions, African American questions, about the whole of Africa, and especially our experiences in America, is a more important and productive use of our creativity. Isn't this our responsibility as Black people living in America?

We will call these, questions about the right questions.

(D)

Intellectual leadership aspects

However, the most important reasons that White people's questions about History are a false issue, is because they divert

Black historians minds away from the most important questions facing Blacks in America, slavery. How are we going to deal with that experience in our history?

On the other side, every Black I know, fears dealing with the subject of slavery, in fact, feels pain when the subject comes up and refuses to give it much thought; this to has a major negative affect on our thinking about our history.

Shouldn't we ask ourselves the question, how could we have any pain related to slavery if we don't know what slavery is about? How can we know what slavery is about if we can't face the issue head on? Are we living in denial?

Is it a matter of having the courage to over come fear of pain? Was Slavery really the only major thing going on in our lives at that time, or is it just something that is blocking our view of something more important?

Therefore the question becomes, can we approach truth while living in denial of our slavery experience? For example, what is the source of the fortitude and knowledge that allows a people to survive living in hell on earth for 246 years, 1619-1865?

Could it be that there was a thing developing in our world that had nothing what so ever to do with slavery, or White people's questions at all, and this thing is our Cultural Spirit? Isn't this Spirit the most important thing about us as a people and our survival?

We only see the negative side of it. However, in a careful research of slavery, once you get around the rush of angry pain, I believe that you will be pleasantly surprised at the large number of positive things that you will find in slavery in a re-definition totally unrelated to White people's questions and way of thinking.

You will from the evidence, come to the conclusion that Black History not only has an intelligence and purpose, but also that we are a great people in our own right, and have one of the greatest stories on earth to tell. Like I mentioned, are we asking ourselves all of the right questions?

This means that since we are the Africans that had the experience, an African Bush way of thinking and doing things must define Africa as well as the meaning of the experience of slavery; aren't we the only ones that can do that? Isn't this reflected in our desire to return to our roots?

But before we can return to our roots, don't we first have to pass through Slavery in America? On the other hand, to travel the time-line from our roots to ourselves, we also must pass through slavery. Can we afford to just skip over that part? Can we think of history without first understanding slavery? Can we understand slavery without first thinking about it?

Shouldn't an African bush way of thinking demonstrate continuity between us and our Ancient bush Ancestors who are Africans south of the Sierra Desert? Don't we need a logical way of thinking of Africa as our Roots? Isn't this the major test to make our history useful and make it real? From this point of view, isn't slavery an important short time period in a history that is thousands of years old?

However, the biggest disagreement I have with some of our Black historians and intellectuals, is that they follow White's thinking, that history should be founded on a scientific approach. While my conclusion is that, for Blacks, for history to be useful, it must be approached from a point of view of Black spirituality. Science and spirituality don't mix very well; I don't care what they are trying to prove in Quantum Physics.

Wouldn't the study of an African way of thinking and doing things as bush intelligence lead to an African Centered world view politically, socially, spiritually, and economically? Wouldn't a useful conception of Black history as a thing to be used, serve a positive purpose in one's life today? And doesn't this lead us into the spiritual world of our Ancestors, our roots?

Are our Ancestors the source of our inspiration, determination, fortitude, and creativity, which are the foundation of a constantly growing Black culture in motion toward our destiny as a people? Doesn't the dynamic energy of our soul come from our Ancestors? Aren't our Ancestors the subject and key players in our history? From this point of view, aren't the Ancestors of Black people live spiritual beings; a dynamic force that transcends time from the far distant past, to the far reaches of our destiny in the future?

In this sense, doesn't African Bush Thinking (Afro-centralism), Black Soul (Black spirituality), Black Ancestors (Black history), symbolized by our Black Culture, show us to be a powerful and beautiful work of art with a beautiful independent Black mind? Doesn't that mean that we should find, and deal with our own questions, including the slavery aspect of our history?

We will call these, questions about Black intellectual leadership.

(E)

Answers to questions aspects

Now Brothers and Sisters, we will turn to the purpose I would like this presentation to serve; first of all, to introduce your beautiful minds to what I believe are our real questions. At the same time, invoke your mind to reach your own conclusions (definitions), especially the value of everything I say about questions in this presentation, and bring your own questions to this presentation also.

But, I especially want this presentation to serve as a means of provoking deep thoughts in your mind concerning the value of our physical and spiritual history, as a means to answer some of the real questions troubling our minds about slavery, spirituality, and the meaning of Black history i.e., the meaning of the Black experience.

And if my parent's questions can provoke you to trust your mind as a pathway to Black creativity in answering questions about slavery, and who we are by using African Bush thinking, I will have accomplished my ultimate goal.

However, if you do not have any questions about slavery and Black history, which is another question all together, on which I will not make any comments, except to say, shouldn't you at least re-think your position in light of the fact that we have a Black precedent? What can history tell us about how that came about?

Being as I made the statement that slavery is our most important question, and an African Bush way of thinking and doing things is the key to an answer, this is the approach I am taking in this presentation. The question becomes, as a historian and writer, how can this be done? Won't we have to turn to African thinking for doing serious research?

I found that Africans are spiritual in nature. They believe that every living thing has a spirit, including ideas and concepts. And that spirit is the sum-total of its aspects. For example, I am a spirit, and have many aspects like father aspect, manhood aspect, and husband aspect etc. etc., the point is that spirits have aspects.

In this sense, according to African beliefs, slavery is a living thing and has a spirit, and therefore has aspects. And this is the foundation of African bush thinking, dealing with the spiritual aspects of a thing. This means looking at the whole picture of slavery, instead of only one part of the picture; for example looking at the physical aspect, and disregarding the spiritual aspect. Won't looking at all of these aspects throw a different light on the issue?

From this point of view, I will now turn my mind, and your attention, to the many questions related to the aspects of slavery as a subject of Black history. And at the same time, demonstrate what I mean by asking the right questions, and the need for defining and re-defining slavery from the point of view of its many aspects.

All of which is to demonstrate the process of African traditional logic, by raising questions and definitions related to Black Salvation; this is the heart and soul what I am trying to get across to the Black community with my questions.

We will call these, questions about the aspects of slavery.

(F)
Cultural aspects

In the 1920s and 30s, did not the Great Visionary Marcus Garvey see that we are a "mighty race?" Did not our Black intellectuals, for instance, Alain L. Locke (Black philosopher) define us as the "New Negro?" What do you think they meant by those terms?

Didn't our Black cultural symbols burst on the world, such as Louis Armstrong (jazzman), and W.C. Handy and Robert Johnson (blues men), along with other Artist' (musicians, writers, painters, and dancers) of the Harlem Renaissance, and culture that has spread world wide and still growing? What does that mean?

Isn't our culture unique in the world in the same way as our African Bush Thinking is unique? How does Rap music fit into that picture? What does this mean to us as Elders of our community? Isn't the Blues a sociological commentary? So is Rap. Isn't Jazz a statement about Social Equality and Personal Freedom, and didn't it come from our hopes and dreams for our future?

Shouldn't what we are accomplishing in the dark, blindly come to light in our awareness, otherwise, how can we define our African values and the role of leadership in our community? Shouldn't we use this Ancestor knowledge and wisdom as our point of departure when we are defining and analyzing everything, especially our history?

Don't we un-knowingly already think this way? Or else, how could we create the culture we now have? Isn't this a good enough reason to trust your mind to be creative in thinking about Black history?

For example, collecting African Art, and not knowing the ritual symbolism that transforms an object into a work of art. Isn't art the result of an Artist capturing the Spirit of values into an image? Isn't this image what we call art? Doesn't art symbolize what we call culture? What is historical culture, but an expression of historical values? Is African art something we are collecting blindly?

Doesn't it make sense, that to accomplish this feat of cultural awareness; we must get to know everything there is to know about those Ancestral Africans that came to America? And also, get to know their descendants all the way down to ourselves? As well as know our Ancient Ancestors in Africa? In this way, can't we tell the story of our cultural journey in America, including slavery experiences, and communicate it to our younger generation?

Wouldn't this really tell us where the cultural symbols of the 1920s-30s came from, and what they mean? And, especially what was meant by the terms "New Negro" at that time? Isn't this a good reason to ask questions about African Bush Thinking?

We will call this, questions of the Cultural Aspects of Slavery.

(G)

Constitution aspects

To begin, my research shows, and there is no doubt between Black historians and most Black intellectuals, that Blacks and Africans are very religious and creative by nature. Being religious is the greatest creative act of mankind. And there is tons of evidence to support this conclusion in African, Western European, The Middle Eastern, and Far Eastern literature.

Blacks have been in America for close to 400 years, 1619-2009 as any black historian will also tell us. My research shows that from 1619, (when we first landed in Virginia) to at least 1800, (after America firmly established its independent Government), 95% of Blacks were not exposed to Christianity. In fact, it was illegal for a slave to be a Christian.

In the North as well as in the South, 5 to 10% of Blacks were so-called free throughout the slave days. And some of them were the only Black Christians.

And what the 5 to10% of us were taught by Whites, 1800-1865 (end of slavery) was not a religion of any sort. This is not to say that Christianity is, or is not a religion, which is a question unto itself, only that the things we were taught was not Christianity.

Then the question becomes, based on our religious nature, what religion did 95% of Blacks believe in for those 246 years?

There were a few Blacks that converted to Christianity in the 1740 "Great Awakening." The majority of Blacks that were free converted to Protestant Christianity after the Civil War in 1865 for a number of reasons; mostly because of its promotion of spiritual freedom, especially the Baptist Church. Are we to believe that as a creative religious people, we were living in a spiritual vacuum for 246 years? Is that even possible in the nature of humanity?

Or, did we use the religions we brought with us, (from Africa) and forge them together to create a new spirituality to especially deal with the conditions we found when we arrived? Isn't this a natural thing for a creative religious people to do?

Isn't there enough evidence in our collective spiritual experience, plus in a look at our present day conduct and attitudes, (especially as shown in jazz and gospel/blues, two of the symbols of our culture) to demonstrate that we did create a spirituality? Doesn't a culture come from one's spirituality, and don't we have a culture?

Do you think it is possible that we used a combination of African Traditional Religious beliefs, which we developed into a system of beliefs that formed a unique spirituality; symbolized by our "ancient ring shout dance," a unification rite of passage which is the oldest and most used ritual by African Americans in our slave days in America?

Couldn't this give birth to a unique Black intelligence and Culture created on American soil to deal with the situations we found on American soil? Is this ring-shout-ritual related to a constitution of beliefs? If not, then what is it related to, and what purpose did it serve?

If the above are true questions, doesn't it make sense that this spirituality was, and is, the source of our fortitude, drive, and determination which sustained us throughout slavery? And it is the unknown driving force in our lives today? If this is the case, why can't we come to the conclusion that this spirituality is our soul, and is African in nature, i.e., we have an Afrocentric Soul?

Isn't there other evidence of a religious divination system called Hoodoo in America, and Voodoo in Haiti directly related to "Dance the Vudu on the cross roads" of our Aja Ancestors in Togo and Benin in West Africa? And especially by the Fon Kingdom, to name one of our Ancestral kingdoms, to show our African spiritual connection. Aren't these examples a foundation of African American's spiritual cosmos?

More importantly, if we have a unique spirituality, doesn't this mean that we have a unique African Spiritual Constitution of our own, which defines who we are as a people unto ourselves? For instance, like the Articles of Faith that define the Black Baptist Church.

Isn't the (written) constitution of the bill of rights, (spiritual values) the soul of America, and everything about Americans flow from that point; who they are, and what they do, feel, and think, and especially their identity as a people? Check out the constitution of the United States of America.

In fact, doesn't every culture in the world have a spiritual constitution (written or unwritten) called religion in most cases? Isn't this the case with African Americans as a people? This doesn't have anything to do with what Dr. King said about integration.

In the slave days and even today for that matter, when those old Black sisters and brothers, our Ancestors(while picking cotton, cutting sugar cane, or dealing with planting rice and other labor intensive jobs) sang songs as, "This little light of mine, I am gonna let it shine", and "I'm like a tree planted by the river side, I shall not be moved", don't you think they were singing about something deep inside of themselves, their spiritual constitution, Soul Power?

Is the source of this "little light of mine" African Bush Intelligence? Where are the "roots" of this "tree" planted by the riverside," aren't they ancient African in nature? What kind of fruit is the tree producing? Doesn't this show that we have a constitution of values we call soul?

Just as important, if we have a unique spiritual constitution, doesn't this imply that we have a unique man-woman relationship, male and female sexuality, and therefore a unique family built of a Jazz Band foundation?

We must come to the conclusion, that we have our own language, moral code, history, philosophy, psychology, sociology, and especially, logic and cultural art. They govern and symbolize our spiritual constitution, and define our sense of Truth, Justice, and Righteousness. Don't they define us as a people?

Doesn't this mean that we have a moral code of ethics of our own? Take a close look into the dynamics of the Black community from an African point of view; can't we see our moral code at work? Isn't this reason enough to ask questions about our history?

We will call this, questions about the Spiritual Constitutional aspect of Slavery.

(H)

Education aspects

Now I want to speak directly to our Brother and Sister Black intellectuals and teachers, concerning the following questions; what do Europeans, Immanuel Kant, George W.F. Hegel, and Friedrich Nietzsche have to do with African Bush Philosophy?

And what do Europeans, Auguste Comte, John Stuart Mill, and Herbert Spencer have to do with African Bush Sociology? What do Europeans, Sigmund Freud, Alfred Adler, and Carl G. Jung have to do with African Bush Psychology? But more important than those questions, what do Greeks, Socrates, Plato, and Aristotle have to do with African Bush Logic?

In light of this, as intellectuals and preachers, do you think each of these subjects should be redefined by giving serious study under the light of African Bush Thinking, especially by our Elder educators, and the Elder leadership of our community?

Or, are our Preachers and Teachers dancing to the tune of undefined words in the name of being politically correct intellectually; all according to the foundation laid out by Eurocentric Thinkers about what is to be taught in public schools, for example John Dewey?

We must ask ourselves, was the American education system designed with Black people in mind? Don't we need more from an education than is offered? How can a person be educated without being taught his History?!!!!!

Doesn't this mean that we must define our own educational needs, especially when we are trying to understand and teach Black history? For example, when the subject is to understand what it means to be a New People of African descendents in the 1920s. Doesn't this mean, as a new people, our history is one of our greatest education needs?

We will call this, questions of the Educational aspect of Slavery.

(I)

Philosophical aspects

Now the question becomes, how do a New People come into reality? Where do they come from? And isn't the answer right in front of our eyes, and is well known by us; isn't the Black, White, and otherwise people in the United States of America called Americans, a New People?

The same thing was, and is taking place in Europe. For example, how the English people came into reality. The answer is that the physical and spiritual unification of the Angle people, Saxon people, and the Jute people, over a five hundred year span was transformed into who is now known as the English people, which was a new people from the time of their unification.

And more recently, how the German people came into reality; both cases are well documented. This is the case in Africa.

Also another good, and less known example is how the Ashanti people in Ghana West Africa came into reality as a new people.

So to answer the question, where does a new people come from? Don't they come from the unification of a group of different people already in reality; like individuals come from a family?

But, don't new people have a new name? If so, what is our name? To my way of thinking, the name should symbolize our definition of our Soul, and or, our experience of unification. Isn't this an African Bush way of thinking about things of that nature? Isn't this what the Ashanti people did?

Beginning in the 1960s, a lot of people began using the names *African Americans* and *Blacks*. I personally like the name Blacks the best, but I use both terms for communication purposes as you can see.

On the other hand, I don't know where the name *Colored People* came from, but I don't like it, nor do I like the name Niggers, that came from the Spanish word for Black, Negro; however, through research, I found that the name "People of Color" and "Children of Africa," was used by Blacks in the 1820s, and at least until 1865. What does that mean as far as Black history is concerned?

But more important than that, isn't the ultimate definition of a people, the name of the values they maintain? Does that mean that no matter what we name ourselves, it will mean the values in our Spiritual Constitution i.e. soul? Aren't these values the ones that came from the unification of our Ancient Ancestor's Values, our roots?

This we will call, questions about the philosophical aspect of Slavery.

(J)

Language aspects

Brother and Sister Elders, now I would like to bring up the issue, once you have Black questions and Black answers, then what? How can an African Bush way of thinking use these questions and answers to further an understanding of Black history? To demonstrate the answer, I will give an example:

One Sunday afternoon while listening to a call in radio talk show, they were discussing the subject of "the value of Ebonics as a Black language;" a subject raised by the School Board in Oakland, California.

A Sister called in with the statement to the effect, "Can we afford to give up Ebonics, isn't it our language, and contains our values?" To me, this Sister asked a powerful question, and gave a powerful answer at the same time.

Her question led me to a series of conclusions. The first of which was to re-study languages, and I found that they have their roots in worldviews. I would like to speak to you Brothers and Sisters very strongly about a re-definition of terms, especially when speaking about Africans and Black Americans using the English language.

Isn't a language built around the "meaning" of things you see in the world, and in yourself? Not only seeing the world, but also seeing yourself in the world. As we have shown, all people don't see the same things. For instance, aren't there words in the African language that cannot be translated into English, which means that those things cannot be spoken about in English?

Therefore, we have to ask the question, do *words have meaning, or, is meaning symbolized by words*? Doesn't meaning come from your relationship with what you see in the world, and words are only a means to identify and communicate what you see?

For example, if Ebonics is a Black language, does it mean that it has its own pattern to its thought structure in Black ideas of the world? Does it also mean that Black's ideas originate in an Ebonics' thought pattern, (Black intelligence) and this means that it is a natural pathway to understanding Black history from the point of an African Worldview? Or to say, does Black history have an Ebonic structure?

Or, is this Sister right; because, Ebonics is a new name for an old language we used to call, "*the way country Black people talk*," or "*broken English*"?

Therefore, from this point of view, isn't Ebonics the language of the values in what we from the South called "Mother Wit" that Black women are born with as a part of their natural nurturing, and contains the most important elements in our history and our values?

This Sister speaking on the radio was not only right in her question, and answer, but at the same time, she laid a foundation I could use to connect African Bush thinking, to the decision to create a third language, and this helped my understanding of what was taking place in Black history.

Isn't this the reason that it is very hard to write about a Blacks world view in "good English" without becoming locked in a European worldview, and you have to continuously re-define words and/or, give them a limited meaning?

In this sense, under the spotlight of African Bush Thinking, doesn't this Sister's question, and answer, further our understanding of the value of Black questions and definition of language as a history research tool? Thus is the value of Black questions and answers. If so, they become a logic-foundation for our understanding of ourselves, and our history.

We will call this, questions about the language symbols aspect of Slavery.

(K)

Identity aspects

From the above point of view, isn't Black history important, in the sense that it brings us into spiritual harmony with our Ancestors? Or to say, doesn't it record the standard of values of our Ancestors we carry in our Soul, and communicated in our language? Isn't it the natural source of our individual, family, and community identity? Isn't studying Black history like having a family reunion with our Ancestors and their values?

Studying Ancestor history is only a means of studying those values and ourselves, otherwise, how can we define our constitution of spiritual values, or ourselves as a new people? Can we be a new people without those values?

For example, I saw a blue eyed blond hair White Jew, and I have seen a Brown Jew, plus, I also saw a Black Jew, each of whom told me in effect that they belong to the Jewish race; and the things that made them Jews, was the religious values they carried in their Souls inherited from their Ancestors. And, if they lose their soul and their spiritual connection with their Ancestors, they lose their existence as Jews. What do you think that means as far as thinking about Black history?

Does this mean that we are Blacks, or whatever name we give ourselves at this time, because we carry Black values in our souls inherited from our Ancestors, and not knowing that those soul values are the things keeping us from knowing our identity as a people? Or, is it because we are new, and haven't been identified yet? Is it a question of the Lost and Redemption of our Soul?

Doesn't losing our soul also mean losing our African Bush way of thinking about things? Why can't we define Black as having the same meaning as Jew, as a means of identifying ourselves? Doesn't this show us that it is not race that defines a people, but it is a spiritual constitution that defines race?

In other words, in an African Bush way of thinking, does History and Ancestors mean the same thing? Or, does the actions and reactions of a people over a historical time line of generations, governed by their own values make them a people?

But, when it is all said and done, what ever name we use to identify ourselves should be defined to mean that Our historical family, and Our Ancestors are the roots of Our self, and the things We inherited from them is our spirituality.

This we will call, questions about the identity aspect of Slavery.

(L)

Ancestor/History aspects

As to our relationship with our African and American Ancestors, here, I am defining history, and our Ancestors, as one and the same thing; using an African definition of history. So for history to have value to us, our Ancestors must also have value to us. So what is the value of our Ancestors?

Have we forgotten the message of Elijah Muhammad, Malcolm X, and Martin L. King; the Father, Son, and the Holy Spirit of the Black movement in the 1960s? Were they not only teaching us what to do, like methods of fighting social and economic racism, and just as important, weren't they also teaching us about ourselves; We are somebody?

Weren't we there in person, and felt the full force of the power of our history in action; and used this power for social defining and re-defining? Didn't we see with our own eyes what was going down at that time?

Does this mean that these three Ancestors are of equal value to us, and symbolize three aspects of the spiritual force of our Ancestor power? Were they unique in that regard?

Or, were they following the course laid out by David Walker, Maria Stewart, and Nat Turner in the 1820s and 30s, who laid the foundation for Black Preacher Leadership, and gave them a voice that they learned from our African Ancestors? People like King Osai Tutu, Priest Anokye, and War Chief Amankwa Tia, who created a new people in Ghana West Africa in 1700, the Ashanti.

Doesn't this indicate to you that we are part of one spiritual force, our historical Ancestors? We are a dynamic force moving through time that can be used to do what we want to do—"we want to do" are the key words. Isn't this the values our Ancestors taught us?

Another way of asking the same question is, haven't we been in America, 1619-2009, 390 years, which equals 19 generations;(20 years per generation) all of which is our Black family, living and dead, and must be honored before we can honor ourselves? Isn't history a "honor your family" history affair?

Shouldn't this family history be the source of the tremendous Black pride we feel, and in some cases, don't know where it comes from? And Brothers and Sisters, through our Ancestors, isn't that pride the pathway link to our Most Ancient African Spiritual Enlightenment? Isn't this another way that our Ancestors are of value to us, along with many other ways as well?

This we will call, questions about the Ancestors/History aspect of Slavery.

(M)

Internal social aspects

There is a lot of talk in the Black neighborhood by young and old; hood talks are saying that Black gangs are dividing the Black community in one way or another.

From the debates going on, is one to think that there is a kind of Black spiritual/intellectual civil war between Preacher followers, and Pimp followers; with one side being called, "social sell-outs, and the other side being called, "social misfits?" Is this really an indication of a division in Black Society?

The question becomes, who is the driving force in the molding of the Black community? Isn't the answer the Black Baptist Preacher, and the Black Pimp Gangster? They both have positive and negative historical qualities as far as Black Society is concerned. Haven't both always had a direct influence on our young people, and therefore, an influence on our past, present, and future society?

For example, do Black gangs have a history? If so, where did they originate? Did we have gangs in the old slave days? If so, is their role different in these times?

A more important question is what role does the Preachers image and the Pimps image play in the community? Are the Preachers all positive, and the Pimps all-negative?

This brings up the question, what is the historical relationship between the Pimp and the Preacher? Is one social and spiritual, and the other cultural and economical? If so, aren't both necessary dynamics in our Society? And who should make the decision?

If you don't think so, then answer the question; what role does this type of social dynamics play in the reality of Black society? Hasn't this taken place in every society in the world from the beginning of time, and is still taking place in every generation of every race? Again, are we asking ourselves the right questions?

According to African Bush thinking, whether a person is a Gangster or not is decided by those who make the laws. For example, we can take the case of America; according to English law, didn't Thomas Jefferson become a gangster when he wrote the Declaration of Independence? Does this mean that America is a Gangster nation?

Don't we have to take into consideration that from the very beginning upon coming to America, there is, and has always been, Jewish gangs, Italian gangs, Irish gangs, Mexican gangs, Chinese gangs, and English Gangs in America? And each one of these people also produced lots of Preachers, and the list covers everybody that came to America after it became a nation? Doesn't this mean that Gangsters and Preachers are the twin pathways to becoming true American?

Does this mean that Preachers and Gangster are a part of the nature of American Society? Or to ask, are Preachers and Gangsters the twin columns that are the foundation of American Society? Isn't this an African Bush way of looking at the role of Gangs in the Black community?

Isn't it a fact that every society in the world has Preachers and Gangsters? Doesn't each African nation think of themselves as Priest' and Warriors, but are called Priest and Gangsters by their neighboring nations?

Doesn't this mean that the best way to decide their values is from what Carter G. Woodson started, define our history and tell our story, especially the part related to slavery and the growth structure of Black society?

Then, can't we see the role of the Preachers and the Pimps in our fight for freedom? Can't we also make a decision about their values to Black society based on their standards, if both fit that profile? Where is all of the division talk coming from? Do we have a division in our Society? If you want to get rid of Black Gangsters, change the way wealth is distributed.

Yet there are certain things that are seemingly a conflict of interest, for instance, unity of purpose between the Pimp and the Preacher. Is that really the case?

Is it possible that the time period from 1619-1865 gave birth to a new people, and slavery did not have anything to do with the process? If the same Black groups, the Akan, the Yoruba, and the Igbo, etc., came to America, and we were the only people here, would we be the same as we are? The question becomes, are we a new people who are on track, on time, and on a pathway leading to our Destiny? Isn't this the real Black question about gangs?

We will call these, questions about the internal-social aspect of slavery.

(N)

Oppression aspects

There is also a belief in the Black neighborhood that there is something wrong with the Black man-woman relationship, the Black family, and the way we raise our children. This is caused by the idea that our family was damaged by slavery based on White people's ideas of those beliefs. Is there a basis in fact for the belief that we were damaged as a people in this way?

Is it possible, that if you take a careful look at African Traditional man-woman relationships, you will find that it has not changed for thousands of years, and compared to Blacks in American man-woman relationships, the same beat goes on today?

It could be that the problems we see in our community between Black men and women come from trying to relate to each other the way we see White people act on T.V. If this is the case, then isn't the question a false issue?

This leaves the question of the "Black Family Damage". This is a legitimate Black question, after all, throughout slavery, Black families were routinely broken up, and members were being shipped to different places.

Isn't there a very interesting twist to our family historical experiences, in that we are very unique? We came into being as a new people without the benefit of an organized family institution. This is the first time in the history of the world, that a people has experienced this type of situation. Is this why most Black and White historians called slavery in America, "The Peculiar Institution"?

How could something be damaged if it didn't exist in that time period? Is it's non-existence, the "thing" causing seemly damage? In ancient African beliefs, it is the community that raises a child; so isn't the community the child's family?

Now, when we take into consideration that we are Africans, and the humanizing principle throughout Africa is, "I exist because my family exists, and my family exists because I exist". So the question becomes, were we damaged from not having a family structure for a long space of time? Can we find the answer in Black history?

This we will call, questions about the oppression aspect of slavery.

(O)

Psychological aspects

Now Brothers and Sisters, I would like to draw your attention to the fact that there is a lot of a special kind of deep seated and very old pain in our Community passed down through out the generations. The question I am most concerned with is, why are we passing this pain down to our younger generation?

Could the pain be caused by the negativity you hear said about yourself, which you don't feel is true, but you don't know what is true, because you don't know your history? Think about it.

Isn't the reason that this pain has not been defeated is that there is a big difference between fighting against something, (what White People feel and think about us) and, fighting for something (what Black people feel and think about ourselves)? Is that caused by a lack of a concept of history?

Does this mean that we have been fighting the wrong battle? Isn't the problem with fighting the wrong battle that we can never see any progress toward reaching our goal, and, this is depressing because we don't know what our goal is? Is this the kind of pain that poisons the growth of our Spirit? Wasn't this the fatal flaw in the Black Panther Party; its spirit was poisoned in the same way. And, while we were successful in the short run, we failed in its long term mission because we were asking the wrong questions? At least as a member, this was my conclusion years later.

On the other hand, isn't through asking the right questions a way that we can achieve the awareness of who we are, and what we were doing as a people? At the same time, and just as important in the process, won't we win our freedom from this old pain?

Now along with that deep old pain isn't there a deep old anger, which motivated us to ask the wrong questions in the first place; especially anger related to slavery itself?

Now Brothers and Sisters, while our pain is rooted in false-issue, even though it is justified, is our anger an obstacle instead of an asset? Don't you think the deep pride of our Ancestors, and of ourselves are more important things to pass down to our younger generation than pain? How can we accomplish this without a conscious history?

This brings Black history back into the picture. Don't you think our younger generation can use some wisdom and knowledge from our Ancestors? In fact, don't we all need it? Isn't this the direction the energy of our anger should take? Fight for what we need to know, and success will follow? Isn't it very clear that what White people think and do is not our major problem? If there is a problem, isn't it us; not fighting to know, and be who we are?

Brothers and Sisters, can't we get down with what's real in our lives and stop the pain in our generation, and free ourselves? And more importantly, free our younger generation from a web of emotional false issues. Won't getting down with Black history rectify the situation?

This we call, questions about the emotional (psychological) aspects of slavery.

(P)

Legal enforcement aspects

Now Brothers and Sisters, since slavery is the subject of this presentation, let's define it from another point of view and see what questions we come up with. For this we need a little history of how it got started legally, which leads us to the English system of White indented servitude (White slavery).

In other words, weren't most of the Whites that came to the early colonies slaves for a time, 15 to 25 years or more? Just like with Blacks, didn't these indenture laws prevent the Whites from buying or selling, by providing punishment for any person who traded with him? He or she was not allowed to leave the master's plantation without permission.

An offense against a White slave was not so heavily punished, as one against a free White; he or she was subject to whipping. If he or she ran away from his term of enslavement it was lengthened on his or her re-capture; and he or she received a certificate of freedom at the end of his term. Wasn't this the case with Blacks when we first came?

Didn't the earliest preserved laws of the colonies show little or no distinction between the White slaves and the Black slaves as to control and management between 1619, and about 1660-70, at which time the laws were changed?

Wasn't the big difference in the new laws that, *Blacks were to be slaves for life, and included all of their descendants forever*? Weren't a few amendments to this law of *slavery for life for Blacks* passed before 1712? And wasn't it at that time when the first elaborate laws to oppress Blacks were enacted; called the Black code?

Also, wasn't 1712 the year that the institution of the Patrollers (Police) was founded, and their sole purpose was to enforce laws designed to oppress Blacks? Wasn't this law completely revised and replaced by a more comprehensive law passed in 1740, at that time called the Negro Law?

And weren't these laws re-enacted after the Revolutionary War in 1776, and lasted until the 1860s-70s, when it was put in the White court system, although amended, where it sill remained the organic Black Code/Negro Law?

Doesn't this mean that as White slavery was fading out, there began to grow two different codes of law, one to control Black slavery, and one to control White freedom, each with its own court system until 1860? And after 1865, each was enforced by one court system, the one we have now, but the purpose of the laws remain the same? If you don't believe it, take a look at the difference between the punishment for possession of cocaine by Blacks and Whites in the twenty-first century.

For example, in the slave days, when a Black broke one of the minor laws in the Black code, didn't the judge and jury, always being plantation owners, find him or her guilty? And the patrollers administered the punishment of beating the Black almost to death, but not so bad that he couldn't pick cotton the next day.

In 2009, isn't the enforcement of the Black Code/Negro Law exclusively in the hands of the police as judge, jury, and administer of the punishment by billy-club beating the Black almost to death right in the street?

And the judiciary system justifies their conduct by saying, "they had a reason", without saying the reason was the Black Code/Negro Law. Isn't Rodney King being beat almost to death in L.A. just one example of what is happening anywhere you look in America? And this is known by every Black and White in America, but don't the beatings go on and on? Now, can't you see the benefit of Black history in understanding the Black experience?

We will call these, questions about the legal enforcement aspects of slavery.

(Q)

Physical imprisonment aspects

Now to get to the point that I am leading to, we must define slavery from still another point of view. For this I will quote the definition of slavery from three sources: (1) given by Webster's New Twentieth Century Dictionary, second edition, 1975. (2) As defined in the Northwestern Ordinance, originally by Thomas Jefferson in 1784 concerning new territory, and passed by Congress July 13, 1787. And (3) the 13th Amendment to the Constitution, proposed by a resolution by Congress, and ratified by the States December 6, 1865. Ending the institution of slavery.

1) Webster's Dictionary..........."slave, ultimately from O. Slav, Sloven, slovo, a word; first applied to captives of Slavic origin in southeastern Europe. 1. *Bond servant divested of all freedom and personal rights; a human being who is owned by and wholly subject to the will of another as by capture, purchase, or birth.*"

2) Northwestern Ordinance "Article VI. There shall be neither slavery nor involuntary servitude in the said territory *otherwise than in the punishment of crimes, whereof the party shall have been duly convicted provided always that any person escaping into the same from whom labor or service is lawfully claimed in any one of the original states, such fugitive may be lawfully reclaimed and conveyed to the person claiming his or her labor or services as aforesaid".*

3) Amendment XIII 1. "*Neither slavery nor involuntary servitude, except as a punishment for crime whereof the party shall been duly convicted shall exist within the United States, nor any place to their jurisdiction.*"

Now Brother and Sister Elders, by law, no matter how we define slavery, isn't the bottom line that it was punishment following being defeated in battle and sold? Doesn't this imply to you that we must define slavery to mean that Blacks were prisoners held on plantation-penitentiaries based on White people's laws, that slavery is the natural outcome of becoming prisoners of war?

If we look at slavery from this point of view, doesn't this mean that today, every Brother and Sister that has, "done time in the penitentiary" been in slavery, and knows everything there is to know about being physically enslaved from personal experience? Don't they know the thinking and feeling of being "captured", the thinking and feeling involved in "doing the time", and, the thinking and feeling of "freedom when they are released?"

For example, there is a question in our community. Why does 10% of the general population (Blacks) represent over 50% of the penitentiary population? Isn't this re-enslavement? Does it have anything to do with a Black Code of Laws designed especially for the control of Blacks back in the 1800s? Doesn't this mean that slavery did not end on December 6, 1865, not even the means of becoming enslaved?

For instance, the 1990s laws governing the use of cocaine I mentioned a minute ago; which is illegal. Young Whites use powdered cocaine which carried a term of a fine, and no penitentiary time. On the other hand, Young Blacks use rock cocaine which carries at least a 5 year term in the penitentiary.

The White politicians that passed the law said, "*They don't want to be seen as soft on crime,*" and Bill Clinton signed the bill. I guess giving whites a misdemeanor charge, and Blacks a felony charge for possession of cocaine, is not being soft on crime for Whites, only for Blacks; what's up with this? Is this a law especially designed for re-enslavement of our hip-hop generation for other reasons?

From this point of view, doesn't slavery mean living under the laws conceived and enforced by "others", Whites in this case? Especially, when we take into consideration that there are no laws in America made by Blacks? Therefore, we must come to the conclusion that we still are legally slaves. So the only question is, are the slave laws better today than yesterday? Does "making progress" change this condition?

Then the question becomes, how do Blacks deal with the situation? What do you think our generation was doing in the 1960s? How were the battles of the 1960s fought? Wasn't it 5% physical and 95% spiritual? Weren't we in a spontaneous state of breaking old slave laws in the name of changing conditions in the plantation-penitentiary we now call "the ghetto?" Did the Black actions in the 1960s stop the double standard laws in the 1990s?

In light of this, shouldn't we clearly define the 1960s, and re-define what was going on in slavery? To really see what slavery was about, shouldn't we take a close look at the penitentiary in the

State of Mississippi; or any other penitentiary where your wife or girlfriend can come and spend some "sex time" as a reward for "good behavior?"

Wasn't this the case on the plantation in the slave days, in the sense that a slave owner would control Blacks with the promise of sex, and at the same time increase his property with the babies born in the process? It's something like running a ranch. Only instead of horses and cattle, they were Black people? But again, was that the only thing going on as far as Blacks were concerned? Doesn't that give us a good reason to look for answers in Black history?

This we will call, questions about the physical imprisonment aspects of slavery.

(R)

External social aspects

Brother and Sister Elders, there is also talk in the hood about racial police brutality. In this regard, I want to point out a couple of little-known facts that may shock you.

Isn't it a fact that throughout the South, where 90% of Blacks lived in the slave days, only 10% of Whites owned slaves, and therefore, had the only economic means to make money in a cotton, rice, and sugar cane economy?

Doesn't that mean that 90% of Whites, (the poor class) and 90% of Blacks (slave's class) were in the same economic class? And we know that slaves, economically speaking, were in the worst of shape. What does that tell you about the economic condition of the poor Southern Whites who owned no slaves, and only owned worthless land?

For instance, throughout the slave days, why do you think Blacks made up songs such as, "I would rather be a slave than poor White trash," and sang them to poor Whites? Didn't this come up in the White house in a conversation between President Andrew Johnson and Frederick Douglas, after President Abraham Lincoln got himself killed; what does that tell you? What does that tell you about the Civil War on the southern side being fought by poor Whites? What were poor Whites fighting for?

Didn't Slave-owners rule Southern poor Whites with an iron hand through the English Lord-Peasant relationship? Isn't that Lordship class based on the wealth of Blacks? Weren't Slave-owners (The Lords) the only government in the South, and controlled all of the wealth? Was there any economic security for Poor Whites? Didn't slave labor rob Poor Whites of any job, or business opportunities? Didn't poor Whites hate slaves for that reason; coming between them and their Lord?

And didn't slaves hate poor Whites, because they would not rebel their position, and naturally joined with Blacks to fight against slave labor? Why didn't they? Wasn't it in their best interest to end slavery?

So there was nothing that slave Blacks or poor Whites could do about their social and economic position. Didn't they begin to spiritually, and sometimes physically fight each other long before the Civil War? Wasn't it in the interest of the plantation owners that poor Whites blamed Blacks, and not them?

Hell, didn't the plantation owner create the police institution for the purpose of controlling Blacks around 1712, and hired all poor Whites as policemen? Weren't they charged with the protection of the thing that kept them poor? And has their job description changed to this very day?

In fact, throughout our history in the United States, haven't these self-same police taken their frustration out on poor Blacks? What happened when the northern cities hired southern Whites for policemen? Isn't this a case of two races of poor folks fighting each other so that they will remain poor? What do you think Black history has to say about that?

The middle class, are only poor Whites that got a raise in pay from their Lord and Master, Wealthy Whites; and now day's, police are middle class, but with the approach and attitude of the slave patroller. In this sense, is there any difference between slave days and now days? Black history can show light on a lot of things going on today.

Even today, poor/middle class Whites can hardly fight for anything themselves, because they spend most of their energy fighting to keep Blacks from getting anywhere socially and economically. Just as it was in the slave days when poor Whites were patrollers (police) of the slave community. And thus are the roots of racial police brutality.

This we will call, statement-questions about the external-Social aspects of slavery.

(S)

Intellectual aspects

Brothers and Sisters, I hear it being said in the hood that White people are stealing things from Blacks spiritually and culturally. Isn't their stealing and acting really an egotistical ritual to not admit to themselves that Blacks have anything of value to offer society.

Or, does this mean that they are seeking a means of controlling the Black Soul? Do they believe that the creator is as great as the creation? Is that possible?

In this way, can't they hate the creator, and love the creation? Isn't this really a case of Blacks indirectly leading Whites culturally when they steal? The question becomes, why do White people have to steal culture in the first place?

Now let's add in some good old African Bush thinking, and see what we come up with. Isn't this a White question or problem? Why should this concern us? If we had questions in this area, it seems to me, it would be, what are White woman stealing from Black men today? And what did White men steal from Black woman yesterday?

But in any case, their stealing expands our culture in the sense that, more people will have our cultural values. In light of this, should we try to stop their stealing? Or, should we help them to steal? But then again, what goes around comes around. For every action there is an equal and opposite reaction. So we must also ask ourselves, what did Black woman steal from White men yesterday? And what are Black men stealing from White woman today?

From this point of view, the question becomes, what are Black and White people stealing from each other? What does all of this stealing really mean to America as a nation? Is this really the definition of Integration? Everybody steals things from everybody else? Is this what Martin L. King Jr. was talking about in the 1960s? Was he naming what was already happening on one level or another, mutual stealing i.e. integration?

By internalizing each others values, are Blacks and Whites really integrating our destinies? Isn't the real question, what are Black and White people learning from each other? And how are they using this information as a weapon to help, or hurt each other?

Or, is our fight only a means to integrate our Societies by not giving up our values, but adding each other's values to their own? Which means, giving America a larger number of values from which to identify itself? Is this an African Bush way of thinking about a mixed ethnic society?

Or better still, are Black people stealing White questions, and White people stealing Black answers to those questions, as a means of getting Blacks to tell them how to control us. If this is the case, isn't this the definition of Black self-imposed intellectual slavery? Therefore, there is only one Black question in this area, whose interest should we serve?

No matter if you are a Black integrationist, or a Black separatist, isn't the answer the same? If this be the case, doesn't this mean that we are using our entire intellectual energy helping Whites reach their goal, without receiving equal help from them in reaching our goals? Which means that our help is at the expense of reaching our own goals? In whose interest is that?

Is this still another definition of slavery? Isn't goal and destiny one and the same thing? Being as the White's goals are for Blacks not to reach our destiny to be free, doesn't this mean that our intellectual power is being used against our best interest? Or, do we get paid for not working on our problems with "welfare checks," and "Black middle class good jobs and pensions?"

On the other hand, maybe it's not that we are working against ourselves; it's that, in stealing White people's problems, we are not working on our own problems? To put this on the right track, we should ask the question, do Blacks and Whites have the same problems? Isn't this what the then-future President Thomas Jefferson was talking about in his book "Notes on the state of Virginia"?

Does this mean that the peace between Blacks and Whites is based on a balanced state of stealing from each other? What is this saying? The point being, neither White people nor racism are our major questions. Our major questions do not have anything to do with White people at all. It's all about us! For example, what are we doing about our history?

We call these, questions about the intellectual aspects of slavery.

(T)

Economic aspects

Brother and Sister Elders, there is also a lot of talk in the hood about economic racism, which is in two forms, jobs, and business capital. First we will deal with the job market. The question is, are we asking ourselves the right questions?

To find the right questions means that we must look at slavery in still another way, which is the relationship between racism and economic class-ism. Isn't it a fact that racism is "social and economic," and class-ism is also "social and economic?" Doesn't this have a tendency to confuse the issue of racism, and this is how the racism game is played by the Democrats and Republicans? Don't they control the Government?

Isn't American society divided into the White rich class, White middle class, and White poor class; and the Black class is divided the same way? Doesn't our survival as a people include much more than just fighting the White man's racism? When we win, then what? Do you believe thereafter everything will be like roses? Like we have died and went to heaven or something?

If we totally defeat racism, aren't we felt in a position like White people class-ism; whereas rich class Blacks think about middle class Blacks, like rich class Whites think of middle class Whites; middle class Blacks think of poor class Blacks, like middle class Whites think of poor class Whites? And the poor class Whites and Blacks think negative about everybody, including themselves? If that *is what it is*, what advantage is it to have a Black president, or have any other color president for that matter?

After saying all that I have said about economic racism, the questions become, do Whites make racist moves to keep us out of the business world? The answer is yes! But are Whites an obstacle to us being in the business world? The answer is no! They only make bumps in the road to the business world. And the same is the case with the job market.

Now Brothers and Sisters, you know these are the realities of the job market and the business world in 2009. Now I ask you in this situation, whose interest is served by keeping racism in the mix. Hint, it is not the poor Blacks and Whites!

We will call these, questions about the economic aspect of slavery.

(U)

Leadership aspects

Brothers and Sisters, what is this noise I hear in the hood about young Blacks not respecting their Elders. In traditional African beliefs, a community needs leadership, and by nature, Elders provide leadership. They seek wisdom, and teach knowledge as a means of governing their community.

And their younger generation held them in high esteem, because they answered questions that were real in their lives; for example, by teaching them who they are and what they are about as people. Which gives them a firm foundation from which to deal with life? Are ghetto Elders teaching anything useful to young Blacks?

In this sense, African Elders lead by teaching history and direction. Shouldn't we take responsibility for teaching our community history and direction? Don't we need a well defined constitution of Black values (Soul) to understand this direction?

And to accomplish this, don't we need an African Bush way of thinking and doing things to give us a clear understanding of the history of our Ancestors? This will tell us what our constitution of values are, and our direction in life, all at the same time.

Doesn't this put us in a position to teach our younger generation who we are, and what we are about as a new people; and this will serve as a firm foundation for them to deal with life. Just as important, we will earn their respect as leaders?

And doesn't our younger generation have the right to demand that their older generation provide this history knowledge for them, which they should inherit as their birth-right? Isn't history knowledge as important as spiritual knowledge as the foundation of their intelligence. Isn't their intelligence their salvation?

Wouldn't this provide a new way of thinking about the nature of the leadership we now need? Isn't this the way to "get down with what is real," and provide the leadership we need to maintain the bond between generations; and keep our values that make us who we are, flowing through time? Isn't this the role of Black leadership?

Now Brother and Sister Elders, do I hear you say "I can't." (For some reason or other) Don't you realize that if any one of our 19 generations in America, especially in the slave days, used those two words, we would not be here? Our Ancestors can maybe understand, "I don't want to," (if you don't think it will work) but never, "I can't".

Brothers and Sisters, aren't we well aware that we have an old and well established leadership institutionalized in the Black Church? Isn't it time for some innovations to be made; not to replace the Black Church, but to expand it with other means of education?

Hasn't, "The age of Black history arrived," but it's not going anywhere? So don't we have to deal with that situation? Doesn't this mean that there is still Elder work to be done in our history education? In this sense, I have some concerns related to our Elder generation, are we half-stepping in our thinking?

We will call these, questions about the leadership aspect of slavery.

(V)
Spiritual problem aspects

So now gray headed brothers and sisters, the question becomes, what is the obstacle to Black people in America developing the kind of historical thinking to fit our situation? Isn't this the thing we must fight to understand? Aren't there aspects of history? Isn't slavery a thing that only the experienced "Old Gray Heads" can interpret? What happened to the "forward look" old warriors of the Civil Rights Movement?

Isn't history an experience of which all of us are a part of, and therefore, it takes a lot of experience in life to understand what history is about? Isn't this our fight? For one instance, fight to make our history and African Bush way of thinking known to our younger generation. Isn't this the last battle that the generation that produced the 1960s is to perform? Isn't this the grey head's swan song?

While not taking anything away from what our generation accomplished in the late 1950s -60s, and early 70s, but being as we already have the experience, and therefore the knowledge, our generation still has one more mountain to move. And believe you me, it is a big fight. Is this being taken care of in colleges; "Black

Studies?" Aren't there people fighting against a redefinition of history, especially Black history? Can we afford to lose this fight?

Didn't I mention in the beginning of this presentation that my ultimate goal is to provoke you to think about questions concerning the value and power of our history? Isn't the question of our history the mountain we must move, and means that we must get this history education thing worked out? Do I hear you say, Isn't America making progress toward equality? The question is, Equal to what?

Isn't the major Black question on the subject to determine if White people are making progress in becoming equal to us in the pursuit of freedom? Should we believe, "becoming equal with White people" is the answer to our questions, concerning who we are, and what we are doing; our spiritual purpose in life? No!

Because I hear you talking about, "I am not spiritually fulfilled." I don't feel as if I have really served any purpose in life. I don't feel self-satisfied." "What has been the meaning of my life?" Those are legitimate questions for old warriors to ask themselves. Ask yourself why you feel that way? Do you think that just maybe it is because we are deserting the battle field before the goal is reached?

Doesn't our spirituality have a purpose designed by our Ancestors, to reach a particular destiny/ freedom; but freedom for what? What is the value of freedom? Isn't the only conclusion that we can come to, is freedom to be who we are, and only then, we will be spiritually satisfied?

No! No! Honored Brothers and Sisters, no people in the world can afford a free-ride on their spirituality, and the meaning of their lives. Isn't it our purpose to serve the cause of our spirituality? And isn't Black spirituality a thing that must be fought for and maintained? What the hell else is more important for an old warrior to be working on before they die?

Spirituality is not free. Everything in life cost something; what do you think is the meaning of ritual sacrifice? And why is it essential in all religions in the world? Isn't our spirituality the only pathway to African 'Bush Knowledge and our Salvation? Doesn't this mean that our spirituality is a tool, and a weapon of salvation? But we can lose it; by losing it I mean, becoming unconscious of it and stop fighting.

Isn't losing our spirituality losing the fortitude, drive, and determination that was powerful enough to bring us through slavery? What are we going to replace it with? What else is powerful enough to deal with the subject of our history? So let's get down with what is real! Isn't it a question of Black salvation?

Do I hear you say, "When we take into consideration of the trading of ideas between Blacks and Whites, our destiny becomes one and the same, and that is our salvation? Is that one of the reasons Martin L. King fought for integration? If this is the case, we have still more reason to keep our traditional spirituality. Where do you think Black ideas come from, our spirituality. Otherwise, where are we going to get something to trade in an integration move?

Listen carefully Brothers and Sisters, are we satisfied living in the comfort zone of doing nothing, while watching soap operas (all of the shows on T.V.)? What does Sex-centered Victorian Romantic ideals (White Spirituality) have to do with our situation anyway? Shouldn't we take a close look at Victorianism before we internalize it as a mate for our soul? Take a close look at war wounds, and the spiritual state of our Black middle class and the things they are fighting.

Doesn't internalizing Victorianism mean that you will have two souls, Black and White? The problem is that they are in conflict with each other, and in the process, if we lose the energy of our soul to this conflict, what are we left with? Nothing!

On the other hand, isn't this also the definition of becoming "schizophrenic," and/or, a "Prozac Junkie?" Isn't this fighting against the control of our spirituality; and we can't afford to lose? And if that happens, wouldn't we be in the middle of a spiritual war within our Soul?

We will call these, questions about the spiritual problem aspect of slavery.

(W)

Unity aspects

Now Brothers and Sisters, every Black I know, including myself, has been saying that the biggest problem in our society is that "we don't stick together." And my father, mother, and grandparents told me that this is what Blacks were saying throughout their lifetime, and that this was also the case throughout slavery. Even my children and grandchildren are saying the same thing; maybe we are on to something here.

So there can be no doubt that we are unified in what we think is the problem, and therefore is our unified question; because there is no doubt that all Blacks think that "sticking together" will solve our problems, i.e. become our savior. So there can be no doubt that "sticking together" is a major question deep in Black people's mind/soul.

Now the question becomes, what do we mean by "sticking together?" Or better still, what is going to "stick us together?" And still further, what purpose is this 'sticking together" going to serve?

To answer that question, I will define the meaning of the title of this presentation to mean, the question is "Black Salvation," and the answer is, "Black History and African Soul." And my intentions were that this presentation looks at the aspects of slavery to demonstrate that History and Soul is an answer to our "sticking together".

We will call these, questions about the unity aspect of slavery.

(X)

Spiritual drama aspects

Early on when I made the decision for my family to make a presentation to your families about Black questions, I found that, before I could begin, I had to define two ideas, "Black" and "History" in my own mind. And in the search for answers, I asked myself two questions,

What will looking back on history tell us about who we are and where we come from, Our Roots?

And what will looking at history forward tell us about where we are going, Our Destiny?

Won't the combination of the two approaches tell us who we are, and what we are doing, Our History?

Because as we see our Ancestors marching through time and generations forward and backwards, won't you see their hopes and desires? Isn't this where you can see their unity of purpose, and their relationship to our hopes and desires? Aren't we a part of a "historical family with a destiny?"

Doesn't this formula allow you to see our Ancestor/History in motion, and doing things, i.e. their experiences? Do you think that a history founded on that premise is useful to us in the twenty-first century?

For an example, we will take the old Black way of thinking about slavery. Blacks were divided into "field niggers and house niggers"; with one being a "sell-out," (bad) and the other as being rebellious (good), depending on which side is doing the thinking. When, according to African Bush way of thinking about slavery, this is not the case. Because each were fighting different aspects of slavery, and both had to win before we got our freedom.

Another example is Martin L. King, Elijah Muhammad, and Malcolm X.; they were great warriors, with each one fighting one aspect of slavery, and the three of them had to win. And so is the case with the other Ancestors mentioned in the text.

The question becomes, will Ancestors/History not only show us all of the aspects we have fought and won, but also the ones we are still fighting, or should be fighting? But more important than this, won't this approach to history show us how our Ancestors were fighting each one of these battles, and what worked and what didn't work, and why, which gives us weapons to fight with as one example of how history can be used today?

This we will call, the spiritual Drama aspect of Slavery.

(Y)

Value of history aspects

Let's take into consideration, the fact that our Ancestors were not only fighting the conditions of slavery, but they were also fighting to establish things like Black culture, society, family, and economics. The question now becomes, will history show us the successes and failures of the past, and at the same time, motivate us to fight in the future?

Won't the history of our Ancestors give us the wisdom and knowledge of the Constitution of the highest valued beliefs of our spirituality? Hasn't it always been, ask the right questions, and trust our beautiful minds to work out the answers?

And in this sense, isn't our history the foundation of our self-esteem? Doesn't self-esteem free our mind from self-doubt, and a free mind can accomplish anything it wants in life, especially our history? And doesn't an African Bush way of thinking about our history free our mind, and isn't this the major reason we should call history, our savior, including slavery?

Don't we need a historical self-esteem to reinforce the self-esteem of the Black community? Isn't it all about the traditional survival plan. Isn't our Black traditional values our most powerful means of putting things in prospective?

Now Brother and Sister Elders, to drive the point home about asking ourselves the right questions, there is talk in the hood that because of Blacks tremendous soul-felt hunger for answers to questions about Black history, that hundreds, if not thousands, are seduced by the myth that they can learn things about themselves, their family, their history, and their origins through DNA testing.

The myth is that, DNA testing can satisfy this soul-felt hunger for knowledge of Black history, i.e. knowledge of self; also your point of origin, and where you fit into the time line of Black history; *Is that possible*?

Don't people consist of a body and a soul? Black history has to do with the soul of a people traveling through time and space, and Souls do not have a DNA footprint. Souls are spiritual by nature, and DNA's nature rests in the realm of the physical body. The case has been made, that the body dies, and the spirit lives forever, isn't that what funerals are all about?

For instance, you can learn if you inherited a bad liver, heart, or lungs, and things of that nature from your Ancestors by using DNA testing, but you can't learn anything what so ever about your spirituality by using DNA testing. What does that tell you? Doesn't it say that there is a hole in that line of thinking? Shouldn't the question be, where did your soul come from? Did it come from a stream of souls traveling down through a time line of history? Where did those souls come from?

For example, if a person says that he has a Christian soul, what is Christianity but a collection of beliefs he lives by. So we have to define soul as a belief system passed down through families and communities. And the history of that soul is the history of the people that have that body of beliefs. Do belief systems have a DNA footprint? No! But do belief systems make you who you are spiritually? Yes! The same is true with the history of slavery aspects and their Afro-centric nature; DNA doesn't fit into the picture. Are we asking the right questions about DNA?

We will call these, questions about the value of Black history.

(Z)
What these questions imply.
Battle zones

With that said, we have come full circle with the meaning of the word Afro-centric. I defined Afro-centralism, as "an African Bush way of thinking and doing things. I also determined that asking the wrong questions was the problem, and we defined Ancestors actions and reactions to life, as the definition of Black history.

However, to get to the implication of the questions as far as a conclusion is concerned, throughout the presentation, we took a kind of spiritual/philosophical approach, and looked at the spirituality of Black's battle zones in, and out of slavery.

And made the case that the content of our Soul is our Ruling Spiritual Ideas; and just as important, these Ruling Ideas are our salvation, as well as the Generals leading us into different battle zones of life. Slavery is only one aspect of Black history. The question becomes, where did those souls come from? Could it be that they came from African Tradition Beliefs?

Anyway Brothers and Sisters, the physical side of slavery was one thing; Whites using force to make Blacks work and not get paid. And this totally negative way of seeing slavery is well known by our intellectuals, historians, preachers, and teachers, as well as the masses of Black people. However, when we look at the aspects of slavery, we can see the whole issue in a more positive light. Y*es, I am using 'positive, and slavery' in the same sentence, because slavery has positive and negative aspects.*

For example, aspects give us a picture of the battle zones Black people were, and are fighting on, as well as the different issues we were fighting for; for instance, intellectual freedom, social freedom, emotional freedom, and the list goes down the aspects that I have mentioned throughout this presentation.

On the other hand, doesn't freedom have aspects also?

So the question becomes, if slavery has aspects, and freedom is the opposite of slavery, shouldn't it also have aspects?

Freedom aspects are what I call Afro-American's Traditional Spirituality (Soul Values), and defines spirituality as an internalized highly valued spiritual belief system you live by, and will die fighting to defend. Aren't those some of Freedom's aspects?

Our history tells us that we won, or, are winning some of those battles, and still fighting others. However, all of them must be won before we win the war; for example, fighting for our history i.e. self knowledge, which is still being fought. Don't you think that it is strange that we have to fight for our history?

This is why I say, Black history has an intelligence and purpose, and is very positive in what it can teach us; and no less is true about our experiences in slavery. And to answer these questions among others, will make a step in turning the Black world right side up in our minds, and deal with any side-effect of slavery on our thinking about ourselves. And then, won't we see the intelligence and purpose in Black history?

Our history not only makes it possible to show the details of the *intelligence and purpose of Black people's lives*, but also, history gives us *consciousness of the power of self-knowledge, and the meaning of Black lives*, and just as important, *makes it teachable*.

Can I get an Amen from our Ancestors, as witnesses that the things that I have spoke to you about in an African Bush way of thinking about things, and the aspects analyzed, demonstrate the beautiful work of art the African Americans have created for ourselves? Doesn't our survival prove this beyond a doubt? Black people lived, and are living one of the greatest stories ever told.

Salute

Lost and Redemption
Flipping the Script

Answers

Brothers and Sisters, at the beginning of this presentation, I said that I wanted to present to you some of the major questions facing the Black community, and why they are important; especially since a Black man has become the President of America.

Like I said, the questions leading to the history from the slave ships, to moving into the White house, has got to be one of the greatest stories ever told, do you agree?

In addition, throughout the presentation, I stated many times that *I wanted to* **provoke you to think about questions of Black Salvation**, and I promised at the end of the presentation, that if you agree with me about the importance of the kind of questions mentioned, I would present some books, and a bibliography which will **provoke you to think about answers for Black Salvation**.

Also at this point, I am going to present the research method I used to seek answers to the Questions of Black Salvation, as well as a bibliography of my research sources. Including, a list of all of the books that I have written, or are works in progress, that are focusing on the answers to the questions mentioned.

So, if you agree that the questions are important to you and the Black community, you will be interested in the answers I came up with in:

Grandpa! Tell us a Story/Drinking from Ancient Wells: Ancient West African Spirituality series-"**The Story of the Game Black People Play-trilogy.**"

It is a memoir of living in the Ghetto, combined with history, which shows the effect of history on living everyday life; this is in the form of the lost and redemption of myself, after I ran away from home on my fourteenth birthday.

And the things that I learned about Black history, and the meaning of life as I spent six years travelling all over the country riding freight trains, robbing, stealing, dreaming of pimping, playing con games, and going to, and getting out of prison. And also, my return home, two weeks after my twentieth birthday; and my redemption by the spirit of Black History.

In that time span, I was growing up to become a man with a strong revolutionary spiritual, social, and economic focus in life. I was not going to let man, or God become an obstacle in my ability to think, if I was to become a man of integrity. *I was challenging everything from Christianity to the Government, even life itself; looking for what is real.*

You will be entertained and enlightened by this sometimes funny, and all the time deadly serious Game I was playing socially, spiritually, and economically. Some would say that I was lost, and that was true in the sense that I hadn't found what I was looking for yet!

On this stage of my Game's performance is where history showcases answers to as many of the questions of Black Salvation as possible, by bringing the knowledge of our Ancestors into the picture of my everyday life. And in the process, I came to know Black History, my Ancestors, and myself. My Ancestors taught me a lot about how we used our Ancient African beliefs to fight for freedom in all of the battle zones of fighting slavery and racism.

Also on this stage, I saw that Black people follow a creative process in working towards fulfilling o*ur destiny, to be free to be who and what we are*, a people creating a pathway to our future. And I saw where *the power of Ancestral wisdom and knowledge* comes into the picture of Black people lives.

In this sense, on this stage, I saw that we are creating our history in space over a time line of Ancestral generations; one generation at a time, as we created ourselves. This is what makes us who we are, Blacks, and this is the true definition of Black people's identity.

Furthermore, hustling on the streets and being in prison, I found that the right questions about my past lead me to self knowledge, which is the heart and soul of con games. If you know how to con yourself, you can con other people. That is why a con man is easy to con, and an honest man cannot be part of a con. Because in conning, the conman reveals how he can be coned.

Using that insight, I could see that we were coned about our history, and that answers to the right questions reveal that we can see the development of Blacks as a new people, and *"break the con"*.

For example, as cold blooded and cruel as slavery was in all of its aspects, slavery was not molding us into who we are, these answers show that we took that experience, and created a force that is transforming American society into the freedom loving nation that it is destined to become. Getting a Black man elected president of the United States is just another step in that direction.

Grandpa! Tell us a Story/ Drinking from Ancient Wells: Ancient West African Spirituality Series shows the logic of this process; and brings a balance between the positive and negative aspects of our history from the far distant past, to the far reaches of our future; by giving meaning to the total historical experience of Black life.

And this is the point this presentation makes, by *using the wrong questions to define the right questions* in thinking about our Afrocentric history. We can see Black people as Artist, creating our history by playing the Game of life the way we do. And the transformation of America, from a slave society to a free society, proves that point. Black people have a hell of a story to tell, because we created and maintained that transformation, and lived that experience.

From this point of view, Grandpa! Tell us a Story/Drinking from Ancient Wells: Ancient West African Spirituality Series has a very positive outlook on where Blacks have been, are today, and will be tomorrow. That is what is shown in The Story of the Game Black People Play; based on Questions of Black Salvation.

Other Books by
Orchester (Hip-hop Grandpa) Benjamin Family

Grandpa! Tell us a Story/
Drinking from Ancient Wells

The Story of the Game Black people Play/Trilogy
Book One: The Game's Soul
ISBN 978-0-9773421-1-2 $24.95
Book Two: The Game's Mind
ISBN 978-0-9773421-8-1 $24.95
Book Three: The Game's Heart
ISBN 978-0-9773421-6-7 $24.95
(Reduced to $15.00 for a limited time)

Questions of Black Salvation/
The Black History and African Soul Story
ISBN 978-0-9773421-3-6 $9.95
(Reduced to $5.00 for a limited time)

The AfroSacredStar Story/
Ancient West African Spirituality
ISBN 978-0-9773421-9-8 $34.95
(Reduced to $20.00 for a limited time)

Order online www.Amazon.com
Or
Order with the publisher at www.SoulViewWorld.com
using (PayPal)

ENJOY

BIBLIOGRAPHY, PAYING THE COST
DOING THE RESEARCH

OK Grandsons, the answer to your questions is to *know what you want, and your mind will lead you to it.* The question becomes, how to pay for it? **Bottom line; *successful thinking depends on how serious you are about what you want.***

I wanted to teach my family Black history because it was not being taught in schools. At that moment, *my mission* in life was revealed to me, and I made a vow then and there (*how I am going to pay for it*) to become an **arm-chair Grass Roots Historian to teach my family the history of the Game, and an autobiographer to teach them the lessons I learned about living Life.** With that vow, I had **chosen what I wanted,** and **my seriousness** led me to *pay for it by doing the necessary research.*

The following bibliography reflects, not only the research done for this book, **Questions of *Black Salvation/Black History and African Soul***, but also was the research source when writing the complete ***Grandpa! Tell us a Story/Drinking from Ancient Wells: Ancient West African Spirituality series***. And it can be used two ways.

It can be used to research the legitimacy of the questions mentioned, and, if some of you who agree that Questions of Black Salvation is Black family and community questions, and who are, or, want to become **arm-chair Grass Root Historians, a**nd who are interested in one man's approach, attitude, and research method in researching the slavery aspects of Black history, I say welcome; **I believe that a new Black history is going to come from Ghetto arm-chair Historians, and it is going to take a lot of us to find it.**

When I decided that I wanted to become an arm chair Grass Roots Historian, I began looking around for an approach to a way to begin to think about it. So I began researching history itself? What does it mean? Where does it come from? Who writes it, and how? What is its value to me? And how do I know what is good research material?

I ran into a book written by Edward Hallett Carr asking the very thing that I was looking for. The title of his book is, "What is history? (Vintage Books, New York, 1961). He made the statement, "The belief in a hard core of historical facts existing objectively, and independently of the interpretation of the historian is a preposterous fallacy, but one which is hard to eradicate." (I strongly recommend that every want-to-be-arm chair Grass Roots Historian buy, and keep a copy of this book near your writing table as I do twenty years later).

Then it dawned on me, that since I lived in the Ghetto, and had been a street Hustler all of my life playing the game for fun and profit, I could successfully interpret Black history by the Games Black people were playing throughout the time we have been in America. Because one thing that I learned from my experience on the streets, is to *recognize, and interpret game when I see it.* And that became *my approach to researching Black History, and I ended up writing* **Grandpa! Tell us a Story/Drinking from Ancient Wells; Ancient West African Spirituality series.**

On the other hand, my attitude is that we have been in America for twenty generations, using twenty years from the birth of one generation to the birth of the next. My grandpa Ben's generation was born in 1880, and that means that my great grandpa George's Generation was born in 1860; great, great, grandpa in 1840; great, great, great, grandpa in 1820 and great, great, great, great, great grandpa in 1800.

Then for example, if I wanted to know what my great grandpa, born in 1800 was doing and thinking about when he was twenty years old in the 1820s, I can research that time period where I would find that he was deeply thinking, and involved on one level or another with the Abolition Movement that was taking place at that time. He and his generation would have been involved in the same Game that me and my generation was playing in the Civil Rights Movement in the 1960s.

And I can carry it still further, all the way back to Africa, when I wrote my fourth book, The *AfroSacredStar Story/The story of a Family Reunion with Ancient African Ancestors*; (however, that bibliography is in the text of that book). In this way, I keep my research personal. It is much easier to become involved when the research becomes a family affair. Thus is my approach and attitude as an arm chair Grass Roots Historian.

Furthermore Brothers and Sisters, I found that each one of the books in my research bibliography, is one "factual dot" in Black history, and my research method is to connect those dots. That was in order to bring out the full picture of what our Ancestors (our historical extended family) were thinking, and doing throughout the time-line of the slavery part of our history in detail. I found it to be spiritually fulfilling, to become acquainted with my Ancestral family.

In this attitude to research, I was not looking for the Author's conclusions, only his researched evidence (facts), and I reached my own conclusions, (truths) by checking with my logic (connecting the dots) to my experiences of playing the Game on the streets.

And a picture emerged of what we were doing in our history, and my interpretation of Black history of slavery from our point of view. My point is that this approach leads *to answers to Questions of Black Salvation that are* found in *Black History and African Soul.*

On the other hand, I call this method, *researching other people's research.* They find the facts, and I found the truths of those facts. For instance, this can be seen in books about "run-a-way slave advertisements;" and this is one of the many ways that I found facts to interpret my conclusions about the slavery aspects of our history. The major point I want to make is, that to do research from any point of view, is to do your research, and interoperate from the area that you have the most experience in life, and you will be richly rewarded with a clearer understanding.

With that said; if you want to go further into the domain of an arm chair Grass Roots Historian, and you decide to use my approach, I will guide you through my bibliography, and show you what to watch out for when doing research.

I strongly suggest that, in the study of any aspect of slavery, begin with the following six books: The first deals with *the question, exactly where in Africa did we come from; to get some perspective on the beginning of the history of slavery.*

Curtin, Philip D. "The Atlantic Slave Trade; A Census:" Madison, University of Wisconsin Press 1967

Herskovits, Melville J.—"The Myth of the Negro Past," Beacon Press Beacon Hill Boston 1941-1958.

Donnan, Elizabeth: The Slave Trade into South Carolina before the Revolution,
Am. Hist. Rev., 33:804-828 1927-1928

The next three books give a perspective of some of our actions, and reactions in how we dealt with the slave days:

"American Negro Slave Revolts:" by Herbert Aptheker.

"A documentary history of the Negro in the United States:"/ Edited by Herbert Aptheker/ Preface by W.E.B. DuBois.

"A documentary history of the Negro in the United States:"/ Edited by Herbert Aptheker/ Prefaced by Henry Gates.

Take a close look at the bibliography of American Negro Slave Revolts, research the researcher and you will find a gold mine of where you can find different sources of letters, diaries, and memoirs of plantation owners, and see the effects of what we were doing to Whites. In the documentary histories also, is where you can study what Blacks were doing, and thinking in our own words.

Follow this up with lots of African Traditional stories, and keep in mind that these are the stories that our ancestors used to educate their children throughout their childhood and puberty years. And check out the relationship between what Africans were thinking and doing, and what we were doing in slavery documentaries. Though there are hundreds of books of African stories, the following three will give you a good start:

Robert S. Rattray, "Akan-Ashanti folktales.

African folktales/ Paul Radin Editor

African Folktales and Sculpture, BolingenSeries XXXII (32). Pantheon Books

The best example that I can give about our approach to researching how our mind works in Black history, is the study of "run-away-slaves" advertised in news papers. For instance, the ones in the time of Ben Franklin's news paper, and see how much you can learn about our approach and attitude from how we were described. You can believe the descriptions, because Whites had to be honest, if they ever hoped to get "their property returned."

From this study, you can learn how we liked to dress, the games we played with White people's minds, the games we played with each other's minds, and just as important, our general attitude and approach to life, and the list goes on and on. Then, look for these qualities in your self, and your extended family generation. This keeps your research on the level of, "It's a family affair", and therefore, personal and on a grassroots level.

And if you study the dairies of southern Whites, you can see their approach and attitude in relation to Blacks, and you can believe that is what they thought at the time. This is another place where they are honest in what they say, and you can see what we had to deal with, then, and now. Then, look in the White community, and see how many of these qualities you find, and how we are dealing with them in 2009. This approach is what makes research so interesting.

As I said in the beginning, even if you are already doing Black history research, making these three studies, Black resistance in slavery, plantation owners letters and diaries, and African traditional stories, is very important for a number of reasons; the most important one being is that they will fortify your spirit when you are confronted with the cruelty you will find happening to your family in researching the slave days. This will keep your anger from blinding you to the positive aspects that were going on at the same time. And in doing research, you want your mind as clear as it can be. I learned this the hard way by having to redo a lot of research.

If you happen to want to research *Questions of* **Black Salvation,** as well as slavery in general, I recommend reading at least one or two authors marked by the sign (**) in the categories that interest you, also if you care to cross check using the other authors in the same category, just to get a rough idea of the substance of that particular aspect. There is no doubt that our history is out there written in books and in other forms, it is only a matter of researching and connecting the dots of truths to get the true picture; that is my attitude.

Black language and education

(**)McNair (Tollette), Wallace Yvonne. "Our African Connection; What We Brought From Home:" Western Images Publication, Inc. Denver Colorado. 1997

Turner, Lornzo D. "Africanisms in the Gullah Dialect." Chicago: University of Chicago Press, 1949

"Ebonics, the true language of Black Folks:" Edited by Robert L. Williams: St. Louis, Mo. Institute of Black Studies, 1975.

"Perspectives on Black English:" Editor, J. Dillard. The Hague, Paris, Mouton 1975

William, William J.: "Black language in America:" Wichita, Kan., Wichita State University, 1973

Wolfram, Walt. "Black-White speech relationships:" Washington, Center for Applied Linguistics, 1971.

Baugh, John. "Black street speech: its history, structure, and survival." Austin: University of Texas Press, 1983

(**) Woodson, Carter Godwin, 1875-1950. "The African background outlined; or, Handbook for study of the Negro." New York, Negro Universities Press, 1968.

.........."The Negro in our History:" Washington. 1947.

"The education of the Negro prior to 1861:" New York, Arno Press, 1968

.........(ed) "Negro Orators and their orations:" Washington, 1925.

(ed) "The mind of the Negro as reflected in letters written during the crisis, 1800-1860." Washington, 1926

Goggin, Jacqueline Anne. "Carter G. Woodson: a life in Black history." Baton Rouge, La. Louisiana State University Press, 1993

Ms Tollette's book, "Our African Connection" first, Chapter VII "On language" and chapter VII, "On Education:" as a kind of foundation for a further study of Black language and education. Ms Tollette is the Sister I heard on the radio mentioned in Questions of Black Salvation.

However, to get into the nature of the philosophy of education in America, I suggest reading at least one of the following books about John Dewey:

Dewey, John, 1859-1952. "John Dewey and American education" edited and introduced by Spencer J. Maxcy. Publisher Bristol: Thoemmes, 2002.

Fishman, Stephen M. "John Dewey and the challenge of classroom practice"/Stephen M. Fishman, Lucille McCarthy. New York: Teachers College Press 1998.

Wirth, Arthur G. "John Dewey as educator; design for work in education, 1894-1904." New York, Wiley 1966.

Afrocentric-ism and Black Spirituality

(**)Diop, Cheikh Anta. "The African origin of civilization:" Translated from French by Mercer Cook. New York. L. Hill, 1974.

........"The cultural unity of Black Africa." Chicago: Third World Press, 1978.

(**)Asante, Molefi Kete: "The Afrocentric Idea." Philadelphia: Temple University Press, 1987.

........."Afrocentricity." Africa World Press, Inc. PO Box 1892 Trenton, NJ 08607.

Browder, Anthony T. "From the Browder File: 22 Essays on the African American Experience." The Institute of Kramic Guidance: PO Box 73025. Washington, DC. 20056 (202) 726-0762

(**)Amen, Ra Un Nefer: "An Afrocentric Guide of a Spiritual Union:" Kamit Publications, Inc., 140 Buckingham Road, Brooklyn, NY. 11226

………"Metu Neter, volume 2: Anuk Ausar: (The initiation system of ancient Egypt; A step by step guide.)"

Williams, Chancellor. "The destruction of Black civilization: great issues of a race from 4500BC to 2000 AD." Chicago, Third World Press, 1974.

Hamilton, Paul L. "Shattering the myths." R.A. Renaissance Publication, PO Box 18323, Denver, Colorado 80218

Lincoln, C. Eric. "Race, religion, and the continuing American dilemma: New York, Hill and Wang, 1984.

Bennett Jr., L. "The challenge of Blackness." Chicago: Johnson Publishing 1972.
Frazier, Edward Franklin, 1894-1962. "The Negro church in America:" New York, Schocken Books, 1974.

Cone, James H. "The spirituals and the blues: an interpretation:" New York, Seabury Press, 1972.

……(**)"For my people; black theology and the black church:" Maryknoll, NY; Orbis Books, 1984.

Lovell, John: "Black song: the forge and the flame; the story of how Afro-Americans spirituals were hammered out."

Baraka, Imamu Amiri: "Black music." New York: W. Morrow, 1967.

Mays, Benjamin Elijah: "The negro's God, as reflected in his literature." New York: Negro Universities Press, 1969.

Washington, Joseph R. "The Negro and Christianity in the United States." Boston, Beacon Press, 1966.
This is a good approach to the 1960s-70s Black movement's Intellectuals, Preachers, and Historian's debate concerning definitions of the Black soul, our Africanisms, and

religion; especially Dr. Asante's "The Afrocentric idea" and "Afrocentricity." Rev. Cone's, "For my people; Black theology and the Black church." Mr. Diop's "The African origin of Civilization." And Mr. Amen's "Metu Neter," who promotes Egypt's spirituality, and is very popular in Black book clubs, especially in Denver Co., and in some cases, is part of a religious movement in that direction.

All of these authors are talking about the same thing, the meaning of the African part of Black Americans. But I think Dr. Asante's books explain it best by giving it a name, Afrocentricity, and defining the meaning of the name in terms of deified histories, and collective consciousness (I call Historical Cultural Self); this pushed his idea into the domain of a self-evident-truth, at least, that is the effect his books had on me. The way he established his ideas are also a good example of the way the Akan deal with ideas, see the Ancient Akan else where in this book.

Civil Rights Movement

(**)Sterling, Dorothy: "Tear down the walls! A history of the American civil rights movement:" Garden City, NY, Doubleday, 1968.

(**) Pinkney, Alphonso. "Red, Black, and Green: Black nationalism in the United States." New York: Cambridge University Press, 1976.

Stokely Carmichael and Charles B. Hamilton: "Black Power; the Politics of Liberation in America." New York 1967.

Floyd Barbour, ed., "The Black Power Revolt." Boston, 1968.

African American intellectual-activists: legacies in the struggle/ Dia N.R. Sekeyi: New York; Garland Pub., 1997.

Baruch, Ruth-Marion, 1922-1997: "Black Panthers, 1968/ Photographs by Ruth-Marion Baruch and Pirkle Jones; Introduction by Kathleen Cleaver. 1st ed. Los Angeles, Calif.: Greybull Press; New York: Distributed by DAP/Distributed Art Publishers, 2002.

"Liberation, Imagination, and the Black Panther Party: a new look at the Panthers and their legacy." Edited by Kathleen Cleaver and George Katsiaficas: New York: Routledge, 2001

"The Black Panthers speak/ edited by Philip S. Foner; with a new foreword by Clayborne Carson: New York: Da Capo Press, 1995

"Picking up the gun; a report on the Black Panthers;" New York, Dial Press, 1970.

(I especially recommend a study of this history by our young generation, so that they don't have to repeat what we have already done. I lean toward the Black Panthers, because I was a member, but there were so many different things going on in the 1950s-60s-70s, and so many Black Authors, that I suggest making it a study in itself, and take a detailed look at the many aspects of Black's actions and reactions in that time period.)

Blacks, Christianity, and the Slave days

(**) Harding, Vincent. "There is a River; the Blacks struggle for freedom in America." New York, Harcourt Brace Jovanovich, 1981.

..........."The other American revolution:" Los Angeles Center for Afro-American Studies, University; Atlanta, Ga.; Institute of the Black World, 1980.

(I would go so far as to say, Dr. Harding's book, "There is a River," was the key to the development of my research direction into the study of Black History back in 1987.

My first question was, "What is the content of this River? Where did it come from? Where is it going? What is its purpose as far as history is concerned?" This gave me a lot to think about.

However, it was later, when I heard Dr. Harding speak on the radio about "Spiritual Transformation." I was lucky enough to catch him in his office on the phone, and he defined the terms for me. This was a big help in my understanding of the role of spirituality in our history; for this I owe him a debt of gratitude.)

Raboteau, Albert J.: "Slave religion; the invisible institution in the Antebellum South." New York, Oxford University Press, 1978.

(This is a great book. Not only in how he deals with the subject, but also his notes beginning on page 323 are a gold mine of authors related to the subject of history and religion for further research; which is also a good source to research into how Black history was handled by Black and White historians before the 1960s.

But most important, he is a good beginning source into the research of the "Ring Shout Ritual," and "Voodoo Divination Ritual:" pages 66-67, 68-73, 245, and 339-40.

However, if you should want to go even deeper into Blacks, Christianity, and the Slave days, as to what Whites were teaching Blacks about religion, I suggest you get the following book, and note, "religious instruction of the Slaves," pages 71-76, and use it as a research guide.)

........"Afro-American Religious Studies." A comprehensive bibliography with locations in American libraries:" Compiled by Ethel L. Williams and Clifton L. Brown. Metuchen, N.J. The Scarecrow Press, Inc., 1972.

Elijah Muhammad, Malcolm X, and Martin L. King

(**)Muhammad, Elijah: "Message to the Black Man." Chicago; Muhammad's Temple of Islam, No.2, 1965.

(**) King, Martin Luther Jr. "Why we can't wait." New York American Library, 1964.

(**) Breitman, George. "Malcolm X; by any means necessary." New York, NY. Pathfinders Press, 1987.

........"The last year of Malcolm X; the evolution of a revolution:" New York, Schocken Books, 1968.

"Teaching Malcolm X"/ edited by Theresa Pery (or Perry), New York, Routledge, 1996.

X, Malcolm. 1925-1965: "The end of White world supremacy; four speeches." Edited and with an introduction by

Benjamin Goodman. New York, Merlin House; Distributed by Monthly Review Press, 1971.

(As you can see by the number of recommendations, I kind of get carried away with Malcolm X. Researching these three leaders is very interesting, especially from the point of an "idea" of the trinity in the organization of Black Preacher leadership, the spiritual dynamics of the 1960s, and insight into the role our Ancestors played in our recent history.)

Richard Allen, David 'Walker, Nat Turner, and Frederick Douglass

Allen, Richard, 1760-1831: "The life, experience, and gospel labors. Microform: to which is annexed the rise and progress of the African Methodist Episcopal Church in the United States of America: containing a narrative of the yellow fever in the year of our Lord 1793; with an address to the people of color in the United States." Microfiche; Chicago Library Resources, inc., 1970.

(**)Payne, Daniel Alexander, Bp., 1811-1893; "History of the African Methodist Episcopal Church:" New York, Arno Press, 1969.

Walker, David, 1785-1830. "An Appeal to the Colored Citizens of the world in one Continual Cry;" edited by Herbert Aptheker: New York; Hill and Wang. 1995.

(**)Walker, David, 1785-1830. An Appeal to the Colored Citizens of the world in One Continual Cry, edited by Herbert Aptheker, New York Humanities, 1965.

Johnson, Frank Roy. "The Nat Turner story: history of the South's most important slave revolt, with new material provided by Black tradition and White tradition:" Murfreesboro, N.C., Johnson Pub. Co. 1970.

Villard, Oswald Garrison. "John Brown": Boston, 1910.

"Life and times of Frederick Douglass:" Rev. Ed., Boston, 1892: Collier paperback; 1962.

(It is very interesting to study Richard Allen, David Walker, and Nat Turner, as related to the ending of slavery, and more insight into the origin of the Black Church, and Preacher leadership, especially if you also research the relationship between the major players.

For instance, the relationship between David Walker, and Nat Turner; the relationship between the Black Preachers of Baltimore MD, and White, William Lloyd Garrison in the early 1830s; the relationship between (Black) David Walker, and (White) William Lloyd Garrison's approach to addressing the issue of slavery; and the later relationship between (Black) Frederick Douglass and (White) John Brown in the mid-and-late 1850s: Which are good examples of seeing the values of Black-history-in-motion: Where as, Richard Allen founded the Black Civil Rights Movement, David Walker founded the Black Voice.

However, to get the full picture of the history of Black leadership, you must take into consideration the role of Black women. You can find out a lot about what Black women were thinking and doing in "The Documentary History of the Negro in the United States," Edited by Herbert Aptheker/ Prefaced by Henry Gates and W.E.B. DuBois. For this study I suggest you begin with):

(**)Stewart, Maria: "Religion and the Pure Principles of Morality. The Sure Foundation On which we must build." Boston 1832.

(As I recall, her works can be found in Herbert Aptheker "A Documentary History of the Negro in the United States."

The most interesting thing is that Maria Stewart was married to David Walker's best friend, and they knew of each other's work, and they were good friends. And when you compare Walker's message to Black men, and Maria's message to Black women, they give good ideas of how Black men and women's minds were in harmony in the early stages of Black leadership. For an example, I will quote from her book.)

".........Many will suffer for pleading the cause of oppressed Africa, and I shall glory in being one of her martyrs; for I am firmly persuaded that God in whom I trust is able to protect me from the rage and malice of my enemies, and from them that will rise up against me and if there is no other way for me to escape, he is able to take me to himself as he did the most noble, fearless, and undaunted David Walker."

(Next, follow the Black Women movements until the1890s-1910, and Mary Church Terrell, Ida B. Wells Barnett, Dr. Rebecca Cole, Rosa D. Bowser, and Frances Jackson, to name a few of the leaders in the National Association of Colored Women; whose slogan was, "lifting as we limb."

Whereas David Walker established the Black men Voice, Maria Stewart established the Black women Voice. Black men and women are still following their approach in the twenty first century.

Maria Stewart was not only the founder of the first Female Anti-slavery Society in the United States on February 22, 1832, and as the first format for the Black Woman's voice in leadership, but she also nurtured it until 1879, some 47 years.

And these 47 years covered the most critical periods in our fight against Slavery, the Abolitionist movement, the Civil War, and Black Reconstruction. And you will see that Black women were in there fighting all the way. In fact, this period produced some of the Greatest Black Women Warriors in our history, and you could see their tradition reflected in the Black women in the 1950s-60s.

In fact, Maria Stewart was the first woman in America, Black or White, to speak before a congregation of men. At that time, women were seen and not heard in 'American Society'.)

King Osai Tutu, Priest Anokye, and War Chief Amankwa Tia
The Ashanti of the Akan Nation

(I bring them into the bibliography picture, not only because I mentioned them in Questions of Black Salvation, but also, because GHANA was such a great inspiration to us in the 1960s Civil Rights Movement.)

(**) Rattray, Robert Southernland; "Ashanti Law and constitution:" Oxford Clarendon Press19 (?)

..........."Religion and Art in Ashanti:" Oxford Clarendon Press 1927.

........."Ashanti", New York, Negro University Press, 1969.

Hayford, Casely: "Gold Coast native institutions with thoughts upon a healthy imperial policy for the Gold Coast and Ashanti." London, Cass, 1970.

Fynn, John Kofi, "Asante and its neighbors, 1700-1807:" Evanston, Ill. Northwestern University Press, 1971.

Edgerton, Robert, "The fall of the Ashanti Empire; the hundred-year war for Africa's Gold Coast (Ghana):" New York; the Free Press, 1995.

(**) Sarbah, John Mensah, "Fanti Customary laws." London, Cass, 1968.

Danquah, Joseph Boakey, "Akan Doctrine of God." London and Redhill, Luthelrworth Press, 1944.

Gyekey, Kwame, "An essay on African Philosophical Thought." Philadelphia, Temple University Press, 1955.

(For evidence of how ancient the Akan-people are, you can turn to a Ghanaian archaeologist, James Anquandah, from the University of Ghana; who is himself an Akan. His book contains the results of his radiocarbon dating figures, which pushes Akan history back some 2500 to 3500 years, and his findings are what can be used as a reference point.)

Author Anquandah, James: "Rediscovering Ghana's past"/ Publisher Harlow, Essex: Longman; Accra, Ghana: Sedco, 1982
(On one hand, the other books give insight into African traditional trinity of leadership and nation building, especially the ritual symbolism of Akan King and Queen mother institutions, once it is understood that the Ashanti are a kingdom in the nation of the Akan speaking people.)
There are a lot of very good books on other Akan Kingdoms by African and European authors for an in depth research in this area.
On the other hand, reading (European) Robert Southernland Rattray, and Casely Hayford books are a good example of a situation where, after cross-checking their very good

evidence with African writers, you will find that you cannot except their conclusion of what the evidence means from an African point of view.

(You must take into consideration that Rattray and Casely are colonial men working towards the control of the people they are writing about for the purpose of "in-direct rule;" which makes their observation honest. In this sense, reading the works of those two writers will give you some insight into the nature of all European archaeology, anthropology, and especially history writers on Africa. And then you can use some of their facts-evidence work in your research.)

New Negro, 1920s-30s.
And Marcus Garvey

(**)Burkett, Randall K. "Garveyism as a religion movement; the institutionalization of a Black civil religion:" Metuchen, N.J. Scarecrow Press, 1978.

"The Marcus Garvey and Universal Negro Improvement Association Papers:" Robert A. Hill editor. Berkeley: University of California Press, c1983-1990.

Garvey, Amy Jacques. "Garvey and Garveyism:" New York, Collier Books, 1970.

(**) Locke, Alain LeRoy, 1886-1954. "The New Negro: an interpretation." New York, 1925.

.........."The Negro and his music; Negro art, past and present:" Arno Press, 1969.

McCarthy, Albert J. "Louis Armstrong." New York, Barnes, 1961.

(**)Jones, Max (Nax), "Louis; the Louis Armstrong story, 1900-1971:" Boston, Little, Brown, 1971.

(**)"W.C Handy, Father of the Blues." (ed) Arana Bontemps, New York, 1941.

(**) Oliver, Paul. "The meaning of the blues." With a foreword by Richard Wright, New York; Collier Books, 1963.

........."Aspect of the blues tradition." New York, Oak Publications.1970.

(For a deeper look at the 1920s-30s-40s, and the idea of New Negro culture, look for books on the Harlem Renaissance, which will give you an idea of Black's creative explosion all over the country in that time period; while keeping in mind, the influences of Marcus Garvey. But also, you can get an idea of how the Great Depression and World War II put a damper on the New Negro until the late 1940s.

And a fun thing to do is to follow the subject of the blues, especially the roles of Thomas Andrew Dorsey and Sallie Martin, who are known as the Father and Mother of Gospel music. This will clear up the question, which came first, the blues, or gospel music? A study into this period of our history gives information far beyond just the subject in question, Blacks as a New People.)

Rap Music

(My research in this area was done in the late 1980s, and beginning of the 1990s. I am sure that a lot more research has been done since then.)

(**) McCoy, Judy, "Rap music in the 1980s a reference guide:" Metuchen, N.J.; Scarecrow Press 1992.

Baker, Houston A. "Black studies, rap, and the academy:" Chicago; University of Chicago Press, 1993.

The unification of the English people

Rosenthal, Joel Thomas, "Angles, Angels, and conquerors, (between the years) 400-1154:" New York Knopf 1973.

........."Anglo-Saxon history: An Annotated bibliography, 450-1066." New York AMS Press.

(**) Hodgkin, Robert Howard, "A history of Anglo-Saxons:" Oxford University Press, 1952.

Finberg, H. P. R., "The formation of England: 550-1042: London; Hart-Davis Mac Gibbon, 1974.

(The English take their history very seriously, which means that there is no problem taking this subject as deep as you choose, and you can learn some very interesting things about them, for example, their Lord-Peasant relationship.)

Bacon Rebellion

(**) Washburn, Wilcomb E., "the Governor and the Rebel; a history of Bacon's Rebellion in Virginia." The University of North Carolina Press, Chapel Hill, 1957.

Frantz, John B., "Bacon's rebellion: Prologue to the Revolution?" Lexington, Massachusetts, D.C. Heath and Company, 1969.

Web, Stephen Saunders: "1676, the End of American Independence." New York, Alfred A. Knoph, 1984.

(This can lay the ground work for a study in Class-ism, showing the tensions between poor and rich Whites, and how it was resolved at the expense of Blacks; which gives some insight into the nature of racism as we know it).

Slave and Indenture Laws

(**) Ballagh, James Cutis, "White servitude in the colony of Virginia: a study of the system on indentured labor in the American colonies." Baltimore, John Hopkins Press, 1895.

Smith, Abbot Emerson, "Colonist in bondage; White servitude and convict labor in America, 1607-1776." New York, Norton, 1971.

(**) Levine, Michael L., "African Americans and civil rights; from 1619-to the present," Phoenix, Ariz.; Oryx Press, 1996.

(**) Chance, William M., "Justice denied; the black man in white America." New York, Harcourt, Brace & World, 1970.

(This gives some indication of the difference between Class-ism, and Race-ism, and how they are being related to the plantation-penitentiary and the Supreme Court relations with Black people. But we must keep in mind that the history of slavery laws are in two time periods meaning, there were two sets of related but some what different laws.)

(1) 1619-1776, laws of the King of England colonial government: And (2) 1776-1865, laws of the American constitutional government. There is a question about the time period between 1865 and 2006.)

Poor Whites/Blacks and National Racism/ Classism

(**)Jefferson, Thomas "Notes on the state of Virginia." 1782.

(**) Henry, H.M., "Police control of the slaves in South Carolina:" Negro University Press, 19(?)

Edited by James O. Breeden, "Advice among masters; the ideal in slave management in the Old South." West Port, Conn. Greenwood Press, 1980.

(**)Bolton, Charles, C., "Poor Whites of the Antebellum South: tenants and laborers in central North Carolina and northeast Mississippi." Durham; Duke University Press, 1994.

(**) Sewell, George Alexander, "Mississippi Black history makers." Jackson; University Press of Mississippi, 1977.

Glassman, Ronald M., "Caring capitalism; a new middle class base for the welfare state." New York St. Martin's Press, 2000.

Westergaard, John, "Who gets what; the hardening of class inequality in the late twentieth century." Cambridge, UK; Polity press; Cambridge, Ma., USA; Blackwell (distributor) 1995.

Hochschild, Jennifer L. "Facing up to the American dream; race, class, and the soul of the nation." Princeton, N.J. Princeton University Press, 1995.

Edited by William M. Dugger, "Inequality; radical institutionalist views on race, gender, class, and nation."

Hoover, Kenneth R. "Economics as ideology; Keynes, Laski, Hayek, and the creation of contemporary politics." Lanham,

Md. Rowman & Littlefield: Distributed by National Book Network. 2003.

(This not only gives some idea of the history of the relationship between Blacks and poor whites and the Police, but also, some idea of the plantation-penitentiary. Thomas Jefferson will broaden your understanding of national racism; some say that he is the father of national racism. There are a large number of authors in this area. Also, there are lots of authors on the foundation of racism/Classism economics, and there is no problem extending research in this direction.)

Black History, Slave-days

Wilkinson, Doris Yvonne, comp. "Black revolt: strategies of protest" Berkeley, McCutchan Pub. Corp. 1969.

Frey, Sylvia R., "Water from the rock; Black resistance in a revolutionary age:" Princeton, N.J.; Princeton University Press.

(**) Stampp, K. M. "The Peculiar Institution; Slavery in the Antebellum South." New York, 1956.

(**) Bancroft, Frederick: "Slave-trading in the Old South," Baltimore, 1931.

Dubois, W.E.B. "The gift of Black folk; the Negroes in the making of America:" New York, Washing Square Press, 1970.

Washington, Booker T. "The future of the American Negro:" Boston: Small, Maynard.

(**) Starling, Marion Wilson, "The slave narrative; its place in American history:" Boston, Mass, G.K. Hall, 1981.

Sobel, Macule. "Trabelin on; the slave journey to Afro-Baptist faith." Westport, Conn.: Greenwood Press, 1979.

(**)Franklin, John Hope, "From slavery to freedom; a history of American Negroes" New York: A. A. Knopf 1947-1967?

(**)Blassingame, John W., "Slave Community." Chicago, University of Chicago Press, 1973.

……..."Black New Orleans, 1860-1880."

(**) Gutman, Herbert George: "The Black family in slavery and freedom, 1750-1925." New York; Pantheon Books, 1976.

(**) Huggins, Nathan Irvin. "Black Odyssey; the Afro-American ordeal in slavery:" New York, Pantheon Books, 1977.

Wright, Richard, 1908-1960, "12 Million Black voices; a folk history: of the Negro in the United 'States." New York, Viking Press, 1941.

"The Trouble they seen; Black people tell the story of Reconstruction:" Edited by Dorothy Sterling. Garden City, NY Doubleday, 1976.

Delany (Delaney), Martin Robinson, 1812-1885. "The condition, elevation, emigration, and destiny of the colored people of the United States:" New York, Arno Press 1968.

Comments to arm chair Grass Root Historians
The following are books I found to be very important to my research of slavery,

Whereas K.M. Stampp's "The peculiar institution," provided important information about the institution of slavery itself; Frederick Bancroft's, "Slave-trading in the old South," deals with problems Blacks had with the breaking up of Black families, and the economic causes. As well as some important information on slave's birth rates, which can be used with importation figures as I did in my book **The *AfroSacredStar Story/The story of a Family Reunion with our Ancient Ancestors*.**

Marion Wilson Starling's book, "Slave Narrative," deals for the most part with books written by Blacks while we were in slavery, and relates to the social, economic, and spiritual conditions of slavery. These, and related slave narrative books can tell a lot about Black's thinking, and doing in that time period.

In the introduction of John Blassingame's book, "Slave Community," he presents evidence that Western Europeans were being enslaved by Arabs in the same time period as we were being enslaved in America; a very interesting book.

On the other hand, Herbert Gutman's "The Black Family in slavery and freedom" is a good source for information on the Black family, and uses of naming practices to maintain links with our Ancestors through the generations.

Whereas, John Hope Franklin's, "From slavery to Freedom", along with Alex Haley's "Roots," are good examples of working with a historical time-line from Africa to the twenty century. There is a lot to be researched in those two books.

SALUTE